The 4th Circle:
How we fall into stress, & how to climb back out

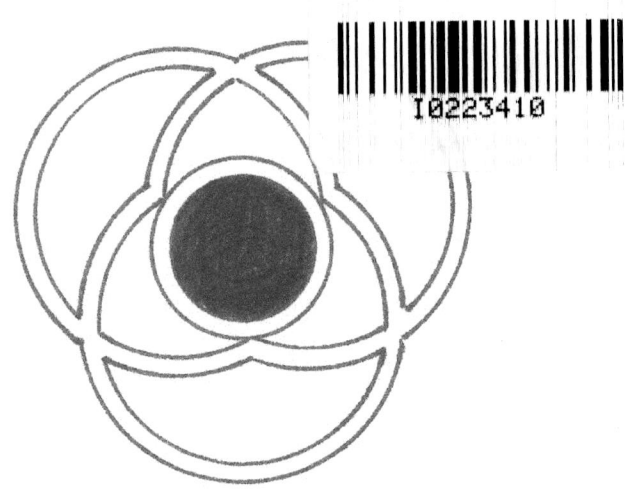

a novel of sorts

Joe Anderson, PhD

The 4th Circle:
How we fall into stress, & how to climb back out

Print on demand version

Copyright © 2015 by Joseph V. Anderson
All rights reserved. No part of this book may be reproduced, stored or transmitted in any form without permission in writing from the copyright owner.

Library of Congress Cataloging in Publication Data
Anderson, Joseph Vernon, 1950 –
The 4th Circle:
How we fall into stress & how to climb back out
Joe Anderson, PhD
ISBN- 978-0-9847120-7-6

1. Stress. 2. Power. 3. Leadership. 4. Business.
5. Anxiety. 6. Fiction. 7. Non-fiction

*Cover design by
Austin Bechtold and Matthew Helf*

Contents

1 Brad

2 Why

3 Hell

4 Won't

5 Assholes

6 Do

7 Love is a Verb

8 Unrequited Love

9 What

10 I, me, mine

11 Tell

12 Change

13 Satan at the Gate

14 Power

15 The Tipping Point

16 Brad's Bloody Eyes

17 So What was the Point?

To Jim, for your words and eyes.

Chapter 1
BRAD

*"Why in the hell
won't these assholes do
what I tell them to do?"*

If you have people reporting to you, you've probably said the same; maybe even a more colorful version of it. I heard just such a rendition this morning from one of the best CEOs I know. It was a thing of beauty, replete with the bluest prose and rambling flourishes of threat and invective. It inspired me to start this book tonight.

That, plus the fact that he had a stroke and died right in the middle of his performance.

It makes you wonder if authority is dangerous to your health.

The facts tell us that the stress involved is gonna kill us, but first, it's going to irritate everyone around us.

- Seventeen thousand, three hundred executives died last year, from the stress of trying to be in control. Seventeen thousand.
- Add to that their 17,000 spouses and 35,000 kids suddenly orphaned and that's 70,000 folks who had a

very bad year because of work related stress. But that's small potatoes, compared to the following facts.
- Before they died, those 17,300 executives crushed 86,500 employees. You know --- crushed --- publicly attacked, humiliated and belittled in a manner that kills the urge to give their best effort. Those folks had a bad year and probably a bad life as well. Not much is worse than working for a fire-breathing, anal-retentive control freak.

But wait. It gets even better.
- Those 86,500 crushed individuals have 4 times more sick days than the non-crushed;
- plus, when they *are* there, they're only about 57% as effective as the non-crushed --- because they're busy keeping a low profile, staying out of trouble and making sure that anything that goes wrong is someone else's fault.
- But that still doesn't seem to help them, because their turnover rate is about 6 times higher than for the non-crushed.

Just ponder that for a moment. That's a lot of transition costs, training costs and ramp-up expenses. Not to mention, legal expenses.

Who do you think sues their employer?
Take your time.
Everybody already knows.
Yep. It's the ones you tried to crush. Some of them fight back --- then you've got one heck of a mess on your hands

--- and your stress goes up yet again, and you end up crushing another truck load of folks who just showed up for work today hoping for a fair day's wages for a fair day's work.

And the parade continues.
- Those 86,500 folks who were crushed by the original 17,300 executives who are no longer among the living --- they turned around and crushed 366,000 more --- because humans do not like to suffer alone. We pass along our misfortunes so that we can have company in our misery.

If you've done the math, you can see that this means that stress grows by a factor of five, while most infections only grow by a factor of 2. So I'm thinking that stress may just be the most infectious scourge known to man.

The contagion often goes on for another iteration or two, but let's stop the process in its tracks and take stock of the situation.

There are 452,500 crushed employees, who emanated from the original 17,300 who died.. So What? Well ...

- 8,700 of them will die from stress within the next 3 years
- 61,500 will change jobs within 18 months
- 295,000 of them have 4 times more absences than normal
- 452,500 of them will be only 67% as productive as normal

- And here's the kicker – those 17,300 hyper-controlling bosses who started the whole process were only 70% as productive as other managers

We lose $13.6 Billion a year due to stressed-out, mismanaging bosses.

And that's just in New York City.

. . .

The actual cost of stress in America is in the Trillions.

Stress will kill you, my friend.

But is doesn't have to be that way. Despite strong evidence to the contrary, I cling to the belief that it *is* possible to be in charge (of a firm, division, department, or work crew) without killing yourself in the process. In fact, I still think that it's possible to have a successful career and a rich, meaningful - and long – life, simultaneously. That's what this book is about.

I serve as Consigliere to America's owners. Business owners. I am part business strategist, part shrink, part drill sergeant, and part pastor. In some respects I play Alfred to their Batman. I get them ready for battle, and sew them back together afterward. We do it mostly via conversation. I was having one of those conversations this morning, when everything spun out of control.

His name was Brad. He was a fine man, and one of the shrewdest entrepreneurs it has been my pleasure to know. Chairman of his church. Beautiful wife. Three great kids, two still in elementary school. And I failed to save his life today.

So instead, I'm gonna try to save yours.

We're going to do that by using "Drift Therapy". We'll drift between fact, commentary and conversation without clear delineation. I'm going to converse with Brad off and on throughout this book. Some of it will be actual conversations we've had, some of it will be conversations I've actually had with other CEOs, and some of it will be conversations I should have had with either one. All of it will be a conversation I _am_ having with you.

Here's the thing about drift therapy, though. It doesn't actually pack itself into a nice neat 2-hour session. Life isn't that sweet. Instead, the conversation reported here rolled itself out over many months during the first year of the Obama administration, when the world was in a massive recession and uncertainty lurked around every corner.

It was a time of acute stress and anxiety, so the language here will be unfiltered and rough, because that is how life is lived, and talked about, in the stress-filled world. About 10% of the CEOs I work with can't speak without obscenities. They put one in every sentence, just to keep their tongue in shape. Another 30% will wax obscene, and creatively so, when they are under pressure. The bulk of CEOs, however, right around 50%, use it sparingly, as an exclamation point, just to let you know when something is serious. And 10% are verbal teetotalers. They never swear. So we know that their inherent obscenity works it's way out in even more creative ways.

Obscenity is a language like any other, so when confronted with a native speaker I adopt the dialect myself so that I can be understood. When you listen to its rhythm you'll notice that it is actually a 3rd party in the conversation.

I've also left in the obscenity because I believe that folks say exactly what they mean.

- ❖ Brad's last words <u>could</u> have been, "How, in heaven's name, do I get these ladies and gentlemen to help me in my quest?"

- ❖ If so, they probably wouldn't have been his last words; because a man who speaks like that doesn't have the same level of stress as the guy who used Brad's words. And he wouldn't have been struggling with that extreme level of stress for the past year or two, and he wouldn't have had a massive stroke, and he wouldn't have died.

No. Brad said exactly what he meant. He didn't care about HOW. He cared about WHY. He saw his employees as assholes out to screw him, not as ladies and gentlemen eager to help him. And he wasn't interested in their help; he just wanted their obedience. He said what he meant, in the way that he meant it, and lived it, and ultimately died from it. So as both a therapist and as a forensic linguist, it's important to retain the words as Brad uttered them.

I apologize if the language offends you, but frankly, Brad's death offends me more; and I'm trying to save a life here. A very important one ... Yours ... So I hope you'll cut me a little slack.

Finally, I should point out to you that I'm a fan of the Socratic method. That is the debriefing method where each answer holds the seed of the next question, not the endpoint of a discussion. I like it for its ability to drill down to the prime cause of a problem; cutting through the conscious and unconscious BS and buffers we place between ourselves and the truth. And I like it for the strategic direction it gives us for pursuing any effort to help one another.

> *"The answer is in the <u>question</u>.*
> *It is not in the <u>response</u> to the question."*

It amounts to the marching orders for the psychic detective. So when Brad blurted out his angry question …

> *"Why in hell won't these assholes*
> *do what I tell them?"*

… he gave us the road map for this book. All we're going to do is walk back through the question one word or phrase at a time. Join me.

Chapter 2
WHY

"It's not the opposable thumb," I said.
"The what?"

"The thumb. It's not the thumb."
"What's not the thumb?" Brad asked.

"The thing that differentiates us from house plants."
"I see," he chuckled. "Ok. I'll bite. What separates us from the lowly house plant?"

"A plant never asks why it ended up in a pot. We do. *'Cogito. Ergo, sum.'* 'I think. Therefore, I am.'"
"Yeh, that may be so," Brad said, "but if you cogito your sum around here one more time I'm gonna stick <u>you</u> in a pot."

I smiled. I got an offer to play for the Chicago Bears & weigh in at over 270 pounds. A guy built like me gets to smile. A lot. "The point is well taken, my friend. No more Latin. I promise."
"Good"

"But the point is valid, none the less. People think. And they think a lot about why stuff happens. And they think a lot about why they should or shouldn't do something – from running a red light to falling in line with one of your edicts. People do things for a reason; which means what?"
"Which means that maybe I need to change my mind about caring why they do things?" hazarded Brad.

"Look, I'm not a psychologist. That crap is just a bowl of oatmeal that wastes my time."

I was stunned by the mixed metaphor. The image of oatmeal clogging a clock overwhelmed me. "Maybe you already know more than you think." I said. How about a little quiz? A bear jumps out of the bushes. ... Quick, what are your options?"

"Run or fight."

"You run?"
"Damn straight"

"You're in the middle of nowhere, in winter, in your Bermuda shorts. The bear has a heart attack and keels over. What do you do?"
"Eat him and make a robe or shelter or some darn thing out of his fur."

"And your favorite movie starlet walks by?"
"Ummm --- Oh! I offer her a little food, shelter and horizontal mambo lessons."

"Think you'll tell her how you killed the bear?"
"It died of old age."

"And that's gonna score you a mambo lesson?"
"Oh, right. I ripped off its jaw bone and beat him to death with it."

"Not bad. But why do you tell her such a whopper."
"It makes me look good. Improves my chances."

"Spring comes. You, the starlet and the mambo offspring are rescued. You write a book. Make millions. You're set for life. What do you do?"

"Ah …I always wanted to do hang gliding."

"Bingo!" I purr. "You should teach at Harvard. You just did a complete rendition of Maslow's Hierarchy of Needs --- considered by some to be the bedrock of motivational psychology. "
1. Immediate Survival – fight or flight
2. Long term survival – food & shelter
3. Affiliation – getting laid, companionship, love
4. Esteem--- find a way to look (or be) worthy
5. Self actualization – the freedom to do whatever you wish

"Not bad" said Brad. "So how do I use it?"

"You don't" says I. "It's bull."
"Bullshit?"

"Well, the academic term is Toro-pooh-pooh. The point is that Maslow's Theory might be a little complex. For instance, where were you at the beginning of the story?"
"Wait a minute." Said Brad. "Is this still Maslow's thing – or are we doing something different?"

"Oh, this is very different I said. "So where were you?"
"With the bear? I was just walking around, apparently looking for an opportunity to play someone's straight man."

"Good" I laughed. "Let's call that place 'POINT A'. Then a bear appeared and you went to …?"
"Point B?"

"Yes!" I chortled. "Point B! Why'd you go to point B?"
"It seemed the functional thing to do," said Brad.
"There was no bear at POINT B."

"Bravooo," I intoned. "That is exceptional. Sometimes we go from Point A to Point B simply because it's the functional thing to do. I'm thirsty, so I get a drink of water. I'm tired, so I turn out the light. We do hundreds of things each day, for no other reason than that we want to get from Point A to Point B. If we over-analyze things we create a real mess."

"Amen" said Brad. He's an old Lutheran.

"But as Ron Poppeil is fond of saying 'But wait! There's more.'"

"Of course there is" said Brad. "There's always more."

" Why'd you lie through your teeth about killing the bear? I asked.

"You told me to" Brad fired back.

"Never did," said I.
"You did too"
"Nope."
"You sure?"
"Yep"
"How so?"
"It's my book."
"Ah… you're right," said Brad. "I made up that whopper on my own."
"I thought so. Why was that?"
"To get her under my bear skin."

"Why would she be willing to do that? You're not all that good looking." His turn to laugh. He had been captain of the swim team at a Big Ten school and still looked the part – 6'2", lean and long muscled. Never, ever, make a joke at someone else's expense.

He took my cue, though, "I told her the story so she'd know I could protect her. By the way, is she in Bermuda shorts, too?"

"It's your fantasy, Bubba. If you want her in shorts, she's in shorts. Doesn't matter to me. But once again, you've hit a home run. She crawled under your skin because she saw you as competent. You were an alpha male. You killed a frickin' bear --- with your bare hands, for God sake. If she wants to survive, she's gonna exercise her expertise as a woman by sidling up to the man holding the jawbone. She's trading her competence for yours. Competence. Say it with me brethren. The 2nd element in this new model is competence. People do things either to exercise their competence, or to make up for NOT having it."

"Wait a second'" mused Brad. "That sounds like a perfect description of practical jokes."

"Yep. They're a classic case of 'I'm incompetent so I'll make you look incompetent too. That way, no one will notice my shortcomings."

"Hmmm" said Brad. "Are you saying that folks who truly feel competent, never pull practical jokes on others?"

"Never is a long time, Brad. I'd feel better if you erased the word 'never' and replaced it with the word 'don't' ".

"OK. Try this. Competent people don't pull practical jokes. Better?"

"Perfect."

"Ok" said Brad. "I got it. People do things to get from Point A to Point B --- or to *enjoy* the trip from A to B --- because of their competence. Is that it?"

"Partially. But we're getting there. Here's the big question. If a bear dies in the woods but there's no one to listen to the stories you make up about it, is there glory?"
"No"

"Why not?"
"Glory needs an audience."

"Yes!! Why?"
"I don't know. And I'm tired. And my head hurts."

"Come on Brad. Buck up. Here's the $20,000 answer. Glory occurs in <u>*YOUR*</u> head. Not the audience's. All they give you is affirmation. Your fertile little brain is what turns it into glory. And what it is that turns the one into the other is beyond us. We don't know. For some people, a private word or a quiet pat on the back are all they need for their glory fix. Others need the roar of the grease paint and the smell of the crowd. Anything less doesn't cross the glory threshold. And you know what that's all about?" I asked.
"What's the right answer here?"

"Acceptance."
"Acceptance," he said. "It doesn't matter whether we're talking about the roar of the crowd or the hum of a single friend, we're all driven by the need for acceptance --- or, wait for it, I remember this --- or by the <u>lack</u> of acceptance in our lives."

"That's it, kiddo."
Brad perked up. "So that's it?"

"Yep"
"So it's a 3 part model as compared to Maslow's 5-parter?"

"Yep"
> *1.* "Function
> *2.* Competence
> *3.* Acceptance"

"That's shorter then."

"By two points. Count 'em."
> "And whose theory is this?"

"Mine"
> "Really?"

"Yep. Journal articles. The works."
> "No kidding?"

"No kidding.
> "So you're a bona fide egghead?"

"Yeh. That's the word I was searching for."
> "I like that," beamed Brad. "I got me a real live academician, here. What else can you tell me?"

"It's bullshit," I said.
> "I'm sorry. The theory is bullshit?"

"Nah. The model is perfectly good. Better than most, in fact."
> "But ……?"

"Let me ask you a question. A bear jumps out of the bushes. Slobber everywhere. You've got 'Lunch' tattooed on your forehead ... At that precise point in time did you say to yourself 'Quick. Should I use Maslow's model or Anderson's to solve this dilemma?' "

"Nope. I just ran like hell."

"Exactly! In the heat of battle, theories and models go out the window. They are pure and utter bullshit."

Brad stood up. "Why in the hell did we spend all that time learning this crap then? I knew it then. It was an utter waste of time. I wasted 16 years of my life in school, learning worthless shit. I've been saying that all my life."

"And you've been wrong your entire life. Sit down, Brad."

He plopped back in the chair. "What?! You just said they were bullshit. I heard you."

"*<u>In the heat of battle</u>* they're bullshit. In the heat of battle. The rest of the time, they're priceless."

"I don't get it."

"I know. A lot of people don't get it. That's why we do such a crappy job of changing behavior. Let me give you a few bullet points on this.

1. It is absolutely crucial that you have a model in your head regarding what makes people tick.
2. That model creates the context in which all of your 'heat of battle' decisions occur
3. But, <u>in the heat of battle</u> you're using gut instinct, not a model. You're just getting from point A to Point B."

Dead pause for a moment, then Brad ventured "Something beats nothing every time, huh?"

"Yep."
"That's a bit shallow, don't you think?"

"Why do you say that?'
"Because of Pastor Peterson" said Brad. Then he grinned "Sin is everything in thought, word and deed that is contrary to the will of God… Geez, that's from my 7th grade confirmation class. Everything's driven by the war between good and evil, between God and Satan."

"Shoot, Brad. That sure sounds like a model to me."
"Yeh."

"Think it's had an impact on the decisions you make?"
"Yeh."

"But I'll bet you rarely think in terms of sin and virtue, especially when you're in the heat of battle."
"You're right"

"But, take a moment to think about your last pressure decision. Did you come down on the virtue side of the fence?"
"The McElhinney deal" said Brad. "Lemme think. Yeh, I guess I did. I left a little extra on the table for him, just to smooth the closing."

"That was good morals, maybe good ethics."
"No," said Brad. "It was just good business".

"Ahhhhh," said I. "Isn't it interesting how those things seem to cluster together? Good morals, good ethics, good business?"
Brad didn't say a word, but you could smell the wheels turning.

I had to ask; "You think the Anderson or Maslow model might have led you to the same decision?"

"I don't know," said Brad "Lemme think. The extra profit was certainly an affirmation of his competence, which put him in the mood to close the deal quickly and smoothly. Yeh – that's your model. And the extra money would certainly affect his self esteem, and it would also allow him to pursue hang gliding or whatever his heart's desire is ... so yeh, Maslow's Theory would have told me to do the same thing as well."

"So would it have mattered which model you used?"

"Wait a minute!" Brad exclaimed, "Did you notice that your model and Maslow's are almost interchangeable? I mean, your competence stuff is clearly imbedded in at least 4 of Maslow's levels – probably all 5. I think the same is true of your function and acceptance stuff too."

"Yeh, now flip things around. You'll see good and evil imbedded in my model, and Maslow's stuff as well."

"Yeh" said Brad. "What's with that?"

"They're all headed in the same direction. Human's all share a sense that there is a moral order to the universe. It shows up in every religion, every philosophy and every scientific school of thought. Even Entropy Theory says that ..."

"I know that one!" interrupted Brad. "That's the one that says that if you run enough random numbers, even *they* start to take on a predictable pattern."

"Pretty close." I said. "And here's the interesting point, regardless of how different the culture, moral order addresses the same issues to one group of folks that it does to another. They all address fairness, opportunity, life, liberty and the pursuit of happiness.

"So then why do we have different schools of thought about why people do what they do?" asked Brad.

"Nuance. Take a look at fairness. Every single religious, philosophical and political system known to man is in favor of fairness. But how do we know something is fair? For instance - you work 8 hours a day. So do I. You sit in an air-conditioned cubicle. I work out in the fresh air. You are conscientious and careful in your work. So am I. You get paid 60% more than I do. Is that fair?"

"Depends on your benchmark." Said Brad.

"What benchmarks?" I asked.

"Well, are you looking at this from the standpoint of inputs or outputs?" said Brad. "Or what about relative measures? Things like equality or proportionality."

"Humph!" I grunted. "You just mapped the 20th century. You built a 2x2 matrix. On one edge you have Equality and Proportionality. On the other you have Inputs and outputs." I drew the matrix on his white board.

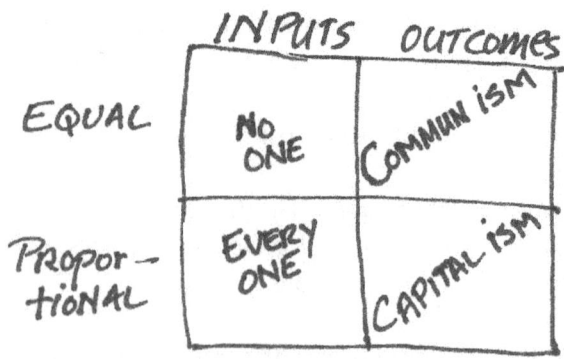

"Notice something interesting," I said. "<u>No one</u>, not a single model is built on the assumption of equal inputs from individuals. In fact, <u>everyone</u>, every religion, philosophy and political doctrine acknowledges that some folks produce more value than others – i.e. – proportional inputs. I find that fascinating."

"Henh" said Brad. He may have been clearing his sinuses rather than agreeing, but I continued anyway.

"And Capitalism and Communism are in large measure simply arguing over the distribution of outcomes. Should we all get the same, regardless of our inputs, or should the more talented folks get proportionately more."

"And we spent 50 years threatening to blow each other up over that? That's a tad bit more than fascinating." said Brad.

"Maybe even 'Important?' "I asked
"Maybe even" he said.

"And here's the part that stuns the ox" I said. We almost blew up the world over that conceptual nuance.

"Hmmm," mused Brad. "So this stuff does something more than give us specific behavioral guidelines. But what?"

"You, my friend are one sharp cookie. Yes, it does a lot more. The model we use is important, mostly, because it frames the situation for us. It tells us what is good, what is bad. It tells us what is fair and what is unfair, what is safe and what is dangerous. So we suddenly find ourselves in the heat of battle, we know what to do --- not by figuring it out on the spot, but by gut reactions that are the product of years of viewing the world from one perspective."

"Like my Uncle Joe" said Brad.

"Who?" I asked

"Uncle Joe. My mom's brother. He was enormous. And hairy. And loud. Oh God, was he loud. You could hear him bellow a mile away. In fact, he was a lot like the bear you conjured earlier. But every time I saw Uncle Joe, I'd run toward him, full tilt. Not away. Toward."

"So your model didn't teach you that big, hairy and loud were dangerous,?" I said.

"A thousand pardons my master," said Brad reverently "The model didn't teach me that big, hairy, loud <u>and human</u> were dangerous. I still had the good sense to run from a bear."

"Yes you did," I grinned. "Nuances."

"Very so," said Brad with a gentle bow.

We hear a lot today about how crummy the American educational system is, as though the problem comes from the input. The critics may have a point. But I've read the textbooks myself. I've looked at the assignments. The content is all there. Literally, we lay the secrets of the universe in front of our kids on a daily basis. And the thing I've found is that most people are like Brad; the material all starts to roll back out of them, processed and surprisingly intact --- *if* you give it a green light to come back out and breathe the fresh air.

- Maybe the problem doesn't exist in the system that puts the knowledge into folks.
- Maybe the problem exists in how we get it back out of them as adults.

"Brad, I'd give you a college degree, just based on what you've told me today. You have processed, and retained, all that material you were so eager to condemn as crap earlier today. It was an incredible display."

Brad was a bit embarrassed by the praise. "Yeh, well, thanks. Who knew?"

"You did, Brad. You did. That's the point. So why did it come out so clearly today?"

"Well in all honesty, you kinda guided me down the primrose path, chief."

"Yeh. But I wasn't putting words in your mouth."

"No. But you were asking a lot of leading questions."

"Yeah. But you were the one with the answers. And, if you recall, you asked some pretty good questions of your own."

Brad thought a second. "Yeh, but ..."

"Waitwaitwait" I said, "Lean forward." He did, whereupon I thwacked him on the forehead with my bird finger.

"Ow. What was that for?"

"That's to remind you that you're a lot smarter than you think you are. Stop plugging your brain with your 'but' "

"My but?"

"Your 'yeh buts'. You've got 'yehbuts' sticking out of every orifice in your head. Stop being your own worst enemy. Give yourself permission to be smart. For some reason, America has adopted a culture of anti-intellectualism. So much so that half the population goes nuts for any politician that puts on his aw shucks hat and makes a couple of dumb jokes about computer nerds. I worry about us, sometimes. I really do."

"You sound like a Democrat."

"No, I sound like an embarrassed Republican."
"Okay" said Brad. "I just gave myself permission to be smart. So now what?"

"Nothing!" I said, "Because you've been smart all along. The only thing that happens when you give yourself the green light is that thinking gets a lot easier, because …"
"Because I've pulled my butt out of my brain."

"Yeh, something like that."
"Heh, heh, heh." Brad just sat there and chuckled for a moment. "This is pretty interesting, Doc."

"Yeh, it is."
"It's like I knew it, and didn't know it all my life."

"Yeh"
"And it all happened just 'cause we took, what's it been, an hour? To shoot the breeze."

"I think we've shot a little more than the breeze", I said, "but yeh, it's been about an hour. Now why do you think you made such strides?"
"Well," thought Brad, "you're easy to talk to. You're safe. You assume I'm pretty bright. At least I think you do. You do, don't you? What're grinning about? What?"

"You think I care."
"Yeh."

"About what you think?"
"Yeh, I do. Am I wrong?"

"No. You're absolutely right. I do."
"Then what?"

"You, my friend, have just discovered the first secret of getting people to do what you want."
"They have to believe I care about them.

And .... ?"
"...and ... what they think."

"Bingo. And you do that by ..."
"...by asking them."

"... and ..."
"... and then listening to their answer."

"Listening." I intoned like a sacred mantra.
"You are such a hambone," he laughed.

"Yeh," I admitted, "but it doesn't change the facts. Folks hate to be invisible. Hate it. With a passion. Which leads to all sorts of bad behavior: sabotaging machines, dogging it at work, or grabbing a gun and going postal. 'Betcha see me now, don't cha?' Visibility is key. Asking them what they think, feel, want --- and then *listening* to their response lets them know they're visible. And when they know that, their behavior gets good."
"It can't be that simple," said Brad. But his body language said, "make me a believer."

So I anointed him with the Hawthorne Effect. "Back in the 1930's, General Electric did an experiment to see how differences in lighting effected productivity in a factory setting. They split their own big factory in Hawthorne Illinois in half. One side got one type of lighting; the other side got a different type of lighting. Researchers were everywhere, measuring activities, asking workers how they felt, what they thought etc. The results? Productivity went up on *both* sides of the factory."

"That's weird," said Brad.

"Not just weird. Downright spectacular. Further research showed that workers were responding to the fact that someone cared what they thought. GE had accidentally made its own employees visible. And productivity took off like a rocket. That's the Hawthorne Effect, and it's been replicated a hundred times."

Brad was impressed. "That's a pretty neat trick."

"Yeh, it is. But if that's all it is, it does you more harm than good in the long run. Workers will get really pissed."

"So what am I supposed to do?"

"Well, you could try *really* caring what they think," said I. "Look, they need to know they're visible when you're making decisions, not just when you walk past them in the morning. Ask them *what* they think. Then ask them *why* they think that. Then *listen* to what they say. And don't pooh-pooh or dismiss what they say. Otherwise you just make them invisible again."

"That's it?" asked Brad.

"Noooo," I laughed. "Far from it. There are as many models about why folks do what they do as there are academics looking for research grants and tenure. Everyone's got a model. You've got psychic, relational and functional bank account models. You've got Gap Analysis and Cognitive Dissonance models. You've got probability, instrumentality and payoff models. Perceptual and enactment models. Nephish and Gnostic models. Attention and valence models. Proactive and reactive, intrinsic and extrinsic, indoor and outdoor models.

They've even got revelatory models, and my favorite – the Evolutionary Psychology model. I call it the caveman model, and it's uncannily useful in making predictions."

"Geeze" was all he could say.

"Yeh. But here's the interesting thing. They all have one thing in common. Every single one of them centers around one thing ----- meaning.   Turns out that mankind wants to know what it all means. What is the meaning of life? What is the meaning of *my* life? What do all these things say about me and my place in the grand scheme of things?

"I don't know, Doc. This is getting' pretty touchy-feely."

I handed him his hat and coat. "Maybe. But I'd suggest you think about it for a while. And when you get a chance, you might want to read Viktor's book"

"Who the hell is Viktor?" Asked Brad.

"Frankl. Viktor Frankl. The book is titled <u>Man's Search for Meaning</u>. Give it a try."

"Yeh, maybe. Thanks Doc."

Chapter 3
HELL

*Beware when thou pointest a finger of scorn,
for the other three pointeth back at thee.*

People talk about what's on their mind. Just not the way they think they do. Pay attention to their words and you'll see that they reveal a lot more about themselves than they do about the topic at hand. It's the "3 finger phenomena". Let's take Brad as a case in point.

- What he said was "Why in Hell won't these assholes do what I tell them?
- But what he might have meant was "I'm in misery (hell) and I feel like an asshole; and I don't know why.

People usually know when they need help, long before they admit it to themselves. So their sub-conscious sends up all sorts of warning flairs. Let's hear it for the sub-conscious. When you learn to listen to it, life gets pretty interesting. The most important thing that Brad said was the word "Hell". People tend to use that word when they feel helpless. In all likelihood, that's a serious cry for help.

Hell
Hell is a desperate place, full of anguished souls. They weep. They gnash their teeth. They cry aloud and heave themselves against the gates and walls. They bleed tears and cry blood. Hell is the stuff of nightmares and honest fears, and folklore out the ying yang. But Hell is very real, isn't it? We know that to be the case, since we've all been there. It is a place of hopelessness, despair, and

claustrophobic panic. It is the place of ultimate suffering, and we have all visited it at least once.

The sad thing is that some of us choose to live there permanently. Those are the one's who have chosen to die, long before their bodies have the good sense to lie down. Brad was one of those people. He was just waiting to lay down. You see, Hell hath another name in our century. We call it the stress/anxiety syndrome.

Stress: Hell by another name
Stress will kill you. Honest to god, it will get you every single time. It will kill you sure as shootin', but first it will twist your guts into a knot, rob you of sleep and ruin every aspect of your life, and the lives of those around you. Then, one day, the stress will move up a notch and take you directly into anxiety. At that point you're almost home. The heart races, the vision blurs, the breathing becomes not just rapid and shallow, it becomes staccato. And eventually, the blood vessel bursts. It always does. If it's in your head, you get the stroke. If it's in your chest, you get the heart attack. Either way, the anxiety ceases immediately. So does the stress. So does the life.

Getting out of Hell
There are only two ways to get out of this Hell. Dying is the first way. That's why suicide is so popular. It works. The pain stops. The Catholic Church has missed the boat on this one for two thousand years. They've been saying that you go straight to hell for all eternity if you commit suicide.

Anyone suffering from stress/anxiety syndrome knows that <u>*they're already in Hell*</u> and that suicide would be their ticket <u>out</u>. Of course, there's the fact that you're dead, so the long-term ramifications of this course of action aren't so good.

The second way to get out of Hell is – buy a gun. Shoot somebody. Anybody. Honest to god, you will feel so much better right afterwards. Going postal is very rational. You know why? Because stress is the result of feeling helpless. And nothing cures helplessness like starring down a gun barrel at someone else. You ain't helpless any more, Bub. Up until they throw you in the slammer and you spend the rest of your life being completely helpless, and hopeless to boot. So the long-term ramifications of plan B aren't much better than those of Plan A.

Notice something about both Plan A and Plan B, though. Both of them work real well, in the short run. They just create an even bigger problem in the long run.

Notice something else. They have something in common. They both <u>do</u> something. Action is the answer. You just have to find a little smarter action to take, that's all. And to do that, you need to understand stress a bit better. So in order to get out of Hell, you have to get into it a little deeper.

Getting into Hell
Let's start by grabbing the bull by the horns. Hell is self-imposed. We made it up.

You heard me right. We made it up. It may be the single biggest tenet of the Christian faith, and therefore of western civilization, and yet <u>The Bible</u>, itself, is effectively mum on the subject. There is no central, cohesive section of scripture that describes, discusses or explains in depth the existence and function of Hell. That's a bit odd don't you think, since the fear of Hell is the very thing that compels folks to cling to their faith in Christianity?

Instead, the few Biblical mentions of Hell are peripheral asides, as though the writers are tapping into current folklore to illustrate a point. In fact, the word "hell", or its various synonyms, is used only 98 times in the entire Bible. That's 98 out of the millions of words in scripture. Miniscule. And of those 98 mentions, only 3 of them refer to a specific place of future suffering and penalty. The rest of the mentions are simply references to the grave or to the state of being dead.

Wow. We made it up. Well, you and I didn't. But we, collectively (mankind) made it up. Actually, the clergy did that, over the course of hundreds of years. Then Dante made it the setting for the Inferno section of his <u>Divine Comedy</u> and John Milton popularized it in his book, <u>Paradise Lost</u>. *That's* where our theology of Hell came from, not from <u>The Bible.</u>

So we made it up. Tell you something else. We're also the ones who condemn ourselves to it.

Getting back out of Hell
Here's the ultimate irony, we can chose to step out of Hell any time we want. All we have to do is stop being helpless, or confused or isolated. If we do something, anything, that changes just one little corner of the world we inhabit, we are no longer helpless. We may never get our former life back, but we are no longer helpless.

Let me explain how this works. The first time I visited Frank, my very first client, for a coaching session, I found him rocking back and forth in his chair, tear-stained shirt, vacant stare, singsong quality to his voice. He was at the edge. His wife had taken the kids and moved out of the house the night before – with all the furniture, to boot. His business was tanking, his marriage was dead, his family gone, his life in complete disarray.

When you are sitting on the bottom of the pit of despair you know how to define helplessness. It goes beyond pain, to complete and utter hollowness. Suicide looks like sweet comfort at a moment like that.

I hauled Frank home. We found an old rollaway bed in the garage and set it up in the master bedroom. And we made the bed. Then we un-made it and I had Frank remake it himself. His assignment for the next week was to make his bed every day. And then he had to study it for 2 minutes, every day, and tell himself that one little corner of his world was now under control. The next week we added brushing his teeth and shining his shoes – everyday. Then noting that the things he controlled had multiplied. The next week we added shampooing and ironing his shirt – everyday etc. etc until he worked his way back to believing that he could have an impact on his own world once again. Then life was worth trying once again, and he re-entered the world.

He never got his wife back. But he found a better one. His business took off like gangbusters, he sold it for far more than it was worth, and pursued a second career in theater, which was actually his first love. We lost touch of each other for 4-5 years, then he called me out of the blue last month and we had lunch. He showed me a picture of his bed, now an overly ornate king-sized 4-poster. "I still make it myself – every single day. I just wanted you to know." That was it. He'd learned how to stay out of Hell. And every day out of Hell is a good day.

I need a model

If you need a model, think of it this way. Hell has three circles. Picture 3 wells with low brick walls. Now picture each one of them as a whirlpool, with just enough suction to pull you under if you were asleep. You can wriggle out on your own if you're only caught in one of them. But if your toe is trapped in two or more of the circles, you'll need some help.

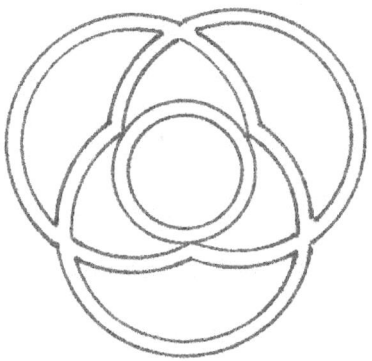

The first circle is <u>Helplessness</u>. It comes from being overwhelmed. You have a sling shot and the opponent has tanks. It doesn't matter how brave or cunning you are, you are going to die, and die ignominiously. The result is Despair. The only way out is to get and use the metaphorical gun. That's what the roadside bomb is. It's the "gun" that can knock off a tank. Do that 2 or 3 times and you'll grow a new crop of heroes pretty quickly. Blowing up one little tank, making your bed every day. Ultimately, they accomplish the same thing --- they both give you hope that tomorrow will be better than today, because you are no longer helpless.

The second circle of Hell is <u>Uncertainty</u>. Take a stadium full of well-educated, white collar Americans, on a moonless night. Now turn off the lights. The beast within them will come out within 17 seconds. Terror, trampling, the works. Absolutely nothing changed, except for one thing. The dark brings uncertainty. For all I know the person next to me could have grown fangs in that 17 seconds. I just don't know. So I get an adrenalin rush, in anticipation of fight or flight. And once the adrenalin kicks in, I have the trembles so bad that if I don't hit someone or run away, I will explode. The same thing happened in the US in the fall of 2008. Someone turned out the lights in our economy. First it was the mortgage market. Then the banking industry. Then consumer credit. The housing market dried up and sales of boats and RVs went to zero. The country literally didn't know what to expect the next day. We couldn't see around the corner. Uncertainty was rampant, and the populace had an adrenalin rush that was so severe that we elected an inexperienced black man to the presidency. Not because he was black. But because he said "I have a flash light, and if you calmly take the hand of the person in front of and behind you, we can find the exit and all get home safely."

Confusion is what keeps us trapped in the second circle of Hell. The ability to see 2 feet in front of you is what gets you out. So learn what lies ahead, or create what lies directly ahead, or simply make it up. It's not the answer itself that matters. It's that someone has an approach to getting out. It gives us just enough hope to quell the adrenalin beast and stuff it back into its bottle.

The third circle of Hell is <u>isolation</u>. We can get through just about any trauma if we have a buddy; someone to talk to, grieve with, and laugh at. But in Hell you have no sounding board. No one to validate your experience, affirm your actions or inspire you to live another day. That's why solitary confinement is so effective. It creates a panic – a silent scream. An endless adrenalin bath, that makes the victim claustrophobic in their own skin. It's why a simple cuddle keeps a baby alive. It's why laying on of hands cures. It's why massage, acupuncture, and even the humble pedicure lift the spirits. Making contact with another human provides the hope that comes from knowing that one more inhabitant of Hell had the strength to survive yet one more day. That's what the head thwack was about with Brad. It was a caress, to calm him in the midst of an emotional rollercoaster ride.

The three circles of Hell teach us two simple things.
  1st – Hell is the act of drowning in one's own adrenalin
  2nd – Hope is the thing that turns down the adrenalin

Combinations
If you're in any two of the circles at the same time, you're in misery.
- ❖ Uncertainty and helplessness = misery
- ❖ Uncertainty and isolation = misery
- ❖ Helplessness and isolation = misery

Your ability to get on top of things is impaired and your willingness to try decreases over time. Most of the stress, anxiety and depression suffered in this world are a result of combinations. And they share a common level of agitation. It is miserable getting caught in a combination. But it is possible to get out, because you're not in the third circle as well. So you've got one foot on dry land and can lift yourself, or be lifted, out.

Education, training and support groups exist for a reason. They keep you from drowning in hell. Same thing with research, strategic and tactical plans and Facebook. They address uncertainty, isolation and helplessness. That's also why churches, political parties and unions exist. Each of them addresses one, or more, of the circles of hell. And those are absolutely crucial because they just might be the one thing that keeps you out of the 4th circle. And believe me, you want to stay out of the 4th circle, because the 4th circle is pure hell. Here's why.

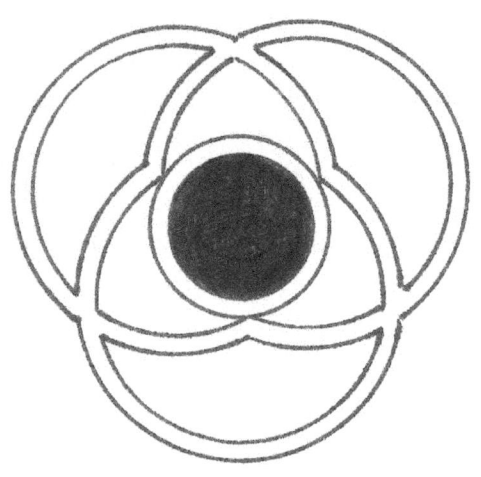

The 4th Circle of Hell – The pit of endless despair
The 4th circle is what gets you. It is the intersection of the other three. If you're suffering extreme uncertainty, can't do anything about it and have no one to talk to about it – the stress shifts to anxiety and the anxiety to utter despair. And that, my friend, is pure hell. It is the depth of hollow horror. The silent scream. The ranting gives way to breathless mouthing and the slack jawed trudging of a dead man walking. It is the absence of all hope or reason. It is madness and death.

If you spend much time in the 4th circle, your life - what little you have left - isn't worth living.

Now, what about your Assholes?

Are they in Hell too? Or is it just you? Do you think that maybe they have a sense of helplessness? How grateful do you think they'd be to someone who reduced the grip of just one of the circles of Hell? Why do you think that unions are attractive to employees?

Can you even imagine what they'd do for the guy who relieves all three? What would **you** be willing to do for that guy?

Be that Guy
Bring hope into the lives of your folks. Teach them to make their bed, every day. Then brush their teeth, iron their shirt etc. etc. Then help them get, and use, their metaphorical gun. Give them some education. Give them a tool. Teach them something they can do, no matter how small. You teach someone not to be helpless and you're halfway home.

Be the flashlight in their dark stadium. Tell them what is two feet ahead or just around the corner. Better still, feed them carrots and help them find their own way in the dark. You give someone a way to cope with uncertainty, and you will have their undying loyalty.

Take the time to listen to your folks. Just listen. Then touch their shoulder, their elbow, of simply shake their hand. People love their sounding board. Be the board. The simple warmth of your presence will give many of them the courage to step over the fence and out of Hell.

If you have been to Hell, even for just half a day, you will understand a very simple rule of life. People will sell their soul to stay out of Hell. That is the core of every religion, and it is the one great truth that underlies leadership.

Getting out of hell
Here's a hard truth to chew on. You will never eliminate helplessness, uncertainty or isolation. Can't be done. The ones who try, earn a posthumous title – martyr to stupidity. So stop trying to do the impossible. Instead, focus on the do-able.

Re-define Isolation – Move from personal isolation to group isolation. A group in isolation has a name. We call it a team. So get folks to buddy up. Put them in work groups. Encourage them to take coffee breaks and lunches together. Give them little trivia questionnaires about each other and give them a free donut if they fill it out together. Give them a uniform, even if it's something as trivial as a t-shirt, or a hat or a 50-cent lapel pin. Any old thing will work. Then poof! They suddenly have an identity, and they are no longer all alone. Then you can become the uber-mensch. You talk about us and we. You talk about them and they and those guys. And those guys are never as sweet as us guys. You don't have to use "The Great Satan" but you get the idea. It's us against the world, fellas. And we ain't alone, 'cause we got each other.

Focus the uncertainty – Don't let the uncertainty be about whether we'll survive, but about exactly how comfortable we will be after this crisis is over. It's not about whether we will win, but by how much. If you don't tell people what to worry about, they will make up their own targets of despair, and theirs will always be insurmountable ones. So get them focused on whether it's better to put square hospital corners in the linens when making a bed. Otherwise they wet their pants in terror over the demon that must certainly be hiding under the bed. So turn on the light – even if it's just a flash light or measly little candle. Show them there's nothing under the bed. Show them where the door is. Help them memorize how to get from the bed to the door in the dark. In other words, communicate – communicate – communicate. The higher the level of uncertainty, the more you need to communicate. Tell them where we are, where we're going and how we're gonna get there. Then tell them again. And again. And again.

Attack the helplessness – We already gave the initial solution to this one. Get people to take action. Make a bed, brush their teeth, pick up the phone, make a sales call, show up to work. Action puts a chink in helplessness, and that breeds hope, and hope diminishes stress to a manageable level. Then you can shift the stress from bad stress to good stress. Good stress comes from a difficult task that you have a 50% chance of mastering. Bad stress sets in when the probability of mastery sinks below 25%. So, teach them a skill, practice with them. Drill them, time them, reward them and/or yell at them. But always let them know that you believe in them. When you do that, you've moved the situation from being one of Risk to being one of Challenge. And everyone loves a challenge.

So, what about Brad?
Some things in life are too privy to share. The conversations between Brad and I on this topic are one of those things. Descending into the 4th circle of hell with a man is an ugly thing, full of fear and loathing. Every demon from the past resurfaces. Every fear and sense of inadequacy papers the walls. A man is not at his best when he is in pure hell. And neither is his guide. No purpose is served, therefore - other than the voyeur's need – by recounting the scene or dialog. Suffice it to say that we discovered that Brad was seriously at risk. We also found that he was brilliant. He'd been getting himself into and out of the 4th circle on a regular basis. He could reason his way out of the Pit of Despair and return to full function and surprisingly jovial demeanor, but, he was apt to slip back

into it on the smallest provocation. I can't institutionalize someone like that. I cannot force them to avoid the inevitable stroke or heart attack. So I have a choice. I can wash my hands of the person and march off in self-righteous dismissal of them as someone unwilling to get well. Or, I can change the rules of the relationship and after full disclosure and waiver, stick by their side as a friend. I don't have much respect for the prissy little boundary setting shrinks, whose biggest concern is their ability to say "Not my fault." So I continued on, knowing full well that there would, most likely, be an unhappy ending.

And the unhappy ending would not be that Brad might die. We all die, even the cheerful ones. The unhappy ending would be that he might not have learned how to live.

Chapter 4
WON'T

"I understand you told them about my time in Hell."

"No. In fact I made a point NOT to tell them about your visit."
   " 'Visit'. I stand corrected. Why 'Visit'?"

"Because you'll be back. Here ... sit down."
   "I don't want to go back."

"Doesn't matter. That is your nature. Have a seat."
   "Crap"

"Yeh."
   "Crap."

"Are you stuttering, or did you just run out of vocabulary?"
   "Fuck you. You've just pronounced my death sentence."

I reached out and cupped his elbow. "C'mon. Sit down, Brad. I'm not pronouncing a thing. I'm just citing statistics. You carry enough stress to fell a horse."
   "But I watch my diet."

"Doesn't matter."
   "Exercise every day."

"Won't help."
   "I take all the supplements, do the green drink, swallow vitamins by the handful. None of those will help?"

"Oh, yeh." I said, "I'm sorry. They'll add a good two, maybe three, weeks to your life."

He slumped into his chair for a moment, then pulled himself to attention. "Okay. I'll just get rid of the stress. You told me about the 3 circles of Hell. I can get out of each one of them. Really. I can. I'm good to go."

"You think so?"
"Yeh."

"Really?"
"Yep."

"You want to keep going, then?" I asked him.
"Yeh. I'm good".

"Okay," I said. "Let's keep going, then. Why do you think they won't do what you tell them?"
"Because they <u>don't</u>. It's pretty open and shut, chief."

I nodded like I was bobbing for apples. "Yeh, yeh, yeh. I know they <u>don't</u>. That's not the issue. The issue is <u>why</u> don't they. Is it that they won't? Or can't? Or don't know who-what-when-where-why? You might want to check your assumptions."

He motioned for me to lean forward like he had a big secret. "Listen. Any ninny can do these tasks. It ain't rocket science, ya know."

I motioned for him to lean in even more, as though my secret was even bigger than his. "<u>Any</u> task is rocket science, Brad, until you master it. Do you take the time to train these folks?"

"Hell, I mean heck yes. They get a full orientation program on their first day."

"So they get specific task training on their very first day?"
"Yep"

"Wedged in between how to find the bathroom and what health benefits do you want?"
"Well, not really wedged."

"Do you do any follow up training after they've been there for a week, or a month?"
"No," he said. "Seemed like a waste."

"Do you show them how their task fits in with the guy in front of them and behind them?"
"Not the guy in front," he said, "but we do spend a fair amount of time on the guy that comes after them in the process. So they know why it's important for them to do things right."

"That's good," I said. "Good. Now do you give them a step by step overview of the whole process, from product conception to service delivery?"
"Not enough time," he said. "Why?"

"Do you give them a written job description?"
"No, Why?"

"So then, you don't have them describe it back to you before you put them into the game?"
"Of course not. Why?"

"You ask them if it all makes sense?"
"No, we don't. Why?"

"Do you have them do dry runs?"
"You mean practice? Role-plays. Dummy work. Simulations?"
"Yeh."
"No time. Why?"

"Do you set a performance goal, a deadline, team lineups?"
"You mean do we do a work flow assessment & chart? No. Why is that important?"

"Do you incentivize them to do it right? On time, under budget, no rework?"
"Absolutely. A paycheck. Now, why is this important?"

"Do you ever ask them if they have an idea of how to do it better?"
"I'd like to know why, chief. I've been asking that question for the past 15 minutes. You're getting nothing else out of me, until I know why you're asking."

Somewhere in the middle there I'd walked over to the window. I gazed at nothing in particular just for professorial effect. "Because I was trying to find out if you delegate things or simply abdicate."
"and …"

"You abdicate. I don't think your folks really understand what you want. So things don't get done the way they should. I don't think they know what to do."
"That's absurd," shot back Brad. "Anybody knows that. …"

"Whoa." I held up my hand. You just illustrated why most bosses are abject failures. Everything they do is based on two ridiculous assumptions:
1. That if they know something, their employees do too.
2. And if they can do something, so can their employees

"Bullshit!" he blurted. "They're not ridiculous, Bub."

"Now it's my turn to call a bullshit." I said, "because it's based on the absurd premise that you are no different than their subordinates."
"Well, I'm not." Said Brad.

I paused, and fiddled with some office doodad for a few seconds to let the room cool down. "Brad, you're a whole lot different than your subordinates," I said. "In fact, I'm not even sure you breathe the same air. You're an entrepreneur. Right?"
"Duh."

"So you were willing to put your life savings, your house and your kid's college education on the line, just to start your own business?"
"Yeh"

"And if we have another meltdown, like the current mess, you could lose it all?"
"Yeh"

"And if you discover that you're not going to be able to meet payroll 3 months from now, unless you make some major changes, but you don't know what to change --- who can you ask?"
"No one"

"Not your banker?"

"Are you kidding? He'd call my loan."

"Your vendors?"
"Grow up. They'd put me on a cash and carry basis. Can't talk to my key employees about it either. They'd put their resumes out tonight and be gone by the end of the week."

"How 'bout the wife?"
"Are you kidding me? She didn't sign on for this."

"Thanks," I said. "You proved my point. You've chosen to live in Hell. You're not passing through. You've pitched a tent. Hell, you've built your own villa. Hell is home to you. All three circles: helplessness, uncertainty and isolation. You bathe in their waters on a daily basis. That is the nature of entrepreneurs. So you tell me ---- in what alternate universe do you suppose that you have anything in common with your employees? They are absolutely dedicated to avoiding, at all costs, the very things in which you happily wallow. They avoid uncertainty like the plague, would rather have a root canal than take a risk, and surround themselves with drinking buddies, neighbors, church committees and PTA so that they never suffer a moment of isolation. So…"

"Maybe we're not that similar?"

"Hmmmmm"
"So maybe my expectations of them are a little over blown?"

"Harrumph. (3 beat pause, rim shot)… so what should you do about it?"
He just started to chuckle as he shook his head, "We're back to the asking and listening stuff, aren't we?" I

nodded and he continued, "You know, you left out the biggest one. I own the damn place. It's my baby. It ain't their baby. If the roles were reversed, that would eat me alive. I can't believe some of them. They knock themselves out as though they owned the place, and for what? They make $19 an hour. 19 bucks. And if I double my profit next year. They'll still be making just $19 an hour. Plus a free trip to Bimini or some other do-dad. And... what are you grinning at?"

"Are those the back stabbing assholes, you're talking about? Or are those the self serving, communist saboteurs? Just curious."

"OK, OK. You got me. Some of my folks are corporate nuns. They've given up everything for this place, but for what?"

"Ah ---- Brad, my son. You pay them far more than $19 an hour. You pay them with the three most important forms of compensation that there are. You pay them with certainty, safety and community."

"What?"

"Think about it," I said. "What happens if they come to work every day, do their job, keep their nose clean and play nice with the others?"

"Nothing. They get paid."

"Every week?"
"Yeh"

"Week in? Week out?"
"Yeh. Every week." Then he started to smile. "Predictably. Consistently. Certainty. I got it. And since I've been micromanaging them, I've also taken all the risk on my shoulders. And they get a nice air-

conditioned office, out of the heat, rain and snow in which to work closely with folks who've become their friends over the years. You're right. I'm paying them certainty, safety and community. I'll be damned."

"Well not exactly," I smiled. "Actually, that makes you the messiah."
"WHAT?"

"The Messiah, my Lord." I intoned. "You single handedly deliver them from the three circles of Hell. By definition, that makes you the Messiah. Well, at least $\underline{A}$ messiah. How's it feel?"
"Stranger than sin," he said as he rubbed his sternum. "I don't think I like being a messiah. Too much pressure."

"Sorry. It goes with the job. Why do you think employees show such an unusually high level of loyalty to their companies, despite the fact that most of them don't actually love their jobs?"
"I couldn't guess." He said, obviously in distress.

"They're buying their way out of Hell. Like buying indulgences from the Pope. You may be one scary mothercurmudgeon, but you're my ticket out of the Hell of uncertainty, risk and isolation. I'm hanging on to you for dear life, no matter what kind of asshole you are."
"Thanks for the theology lesson," he grumbled, obviously feeling a little better. "One little question. Why are Christians so hot to get to heaven? Sounds pretty grim. An eternity of stroking a God who obviously has major ego needs, stuck singing in some celestial choir for all time. Every day, all day for all time. Geeze."

"I didn't say they were hot to get into heaven. I said they were hot to stay out of Hell. But consider this – if you're forced to spend eternity doing the same thing every day, in a group --- maybe that is heaven for most folks. No uncertainty. No risk. And lots of company."

"So how do you find those people?"

"Which ones?"

"Does it matter? Whichever ones I need?"

I grinned. "Yeh. It matters. We're not going to waste time on this one though."

He winced. "Why not? It seems important."

"Oh it is." I agreed. "Very important. But there are a 100 books on the subject already. You don't need me rehashing old ground.
- Figure out the skills needed for the position.
- Write down the keys to success in that position.
- Build your talent pool based on skill,
- then weed it back down based on attitude and the other keys to success.

That's your short list. Then keep your mouth shut during the interview."

"What?"

"Keep your mouth shut. Ask a leading question, one that requires a few complete sentences as an answer. Then shut up. Most bosses make the mistake of giving away the answers and simply watching whether the applicant nods their head or not. 'This firm believes in Truth, Justice and the American Way Mr. Applicant. What about you?" Unless he's brain dead, Mr. Applicant will bound from his chair shouting, 'That's uncanny. I believe the same dog gone thing. It's nice to be home!"

"I get it. I get it." he chuckled as he held his hand up to signal me to stop.

"Yeh. And you also got the <u>Reader's Digest</u> version of a 100 books on recruiting and interviewing in 10 minutes" I said. "So let's move on."

"Okay, Mr. Digest, thanks a lot. But how do I turn them into folks who WILL do what they need to do?"

"Ah, repetition. It is the soul of teaching." I held up a finger, 'Tell them exactly what they need to do."

"I do."

"You don't. Instead, you tell them *approximately* what you want them to do, then spend the rest of the time getting angry at their ignorance. Save yourself the stress and tell them the specifics." I held up another finger. "Discuss how you're going to know if they're doing a good job." Another finger, "Then unleash them. Give 'em a green light to wow you."

"Whoa. Whoa. Whoa." Blurted Brad. "Back up a bit, Pardner. What's that thing about how I'm gonna know…?"

"Whether they're doing a good job." I completed his thought. "Yeh. Well when was the last time you played 'Beat the Water Cooler?"

"Beat the what?"

"The Water Cooler. You never played Beat the Water Cooler?"

"Never even heard of it" he leaned forward. "How's it go?"

"You got a hundred?" I asked. "Yeh? Well fork it over." I put it on the table between us. "Here's how you play. You tell your folks that you've got a pocket full of hundreds that you want to give away. And all they've got to do is sit down for a chat, and tell you how they beat the water cooler."

"You're serious?" Brad asked.

"Dead damn, I am," said I. "The first guy comes in and tells you he hasn't missed a day of work in two years. You say 'Sorry. Neither has the water cooler. NEXT!' The next guy loses too; 'cause all he has to offer is that he's been on time every day for the past 10 years. The third one's a gal with an earnest face. She fares no better. Seems she's never stolen anything from you – not even a paper clip. Sorry, neither has the water cooler. And so it goes throughout the morning."

"This is for real?" Brad asked.

"Real as a heart attack," I responded. "After talking to ten of them, you have a team meeting, and they want to know how in the hell they're supposed to beat the water cooler. That's your AHA moment. Take it. 'I'm delighted you asked,' says you. You just have to do something the water cooler can't. Have a new idea, save money, make more money. Help somebody. Volunteer. Go learn something, on your own.' Let it sit out there for a few beats. Then just say, "Let's do this again next Tuesday, shall we?" And bring lots of hundreds next Tuesday. ---- That's how you play Beat the Water Cooler. Great thing is --- you always win. Especially if they do.

Brad was up fiddling with every do-dad on my bookshelves. "So all of this goes back to what a schlep I am?" he asked. "Clearly, my assumptions might have been in error."

"Could be. And what do we learn from that?" I asked.

"That I can never really know another guy's motivation. So I get myself in trouble anytime I try."

"Well, almost," I said. Anytime you're in relationship with someone you're better served to *ask* them why they did or did not do something, or why they feel one way versus another. That's always a good idea, because guessing wrong can really screw up the relationships."

"Got it." He paused, then a light went on in Georgia, "But if I'm *not* already in a relationship with them, it's a good idea to assume what their motivations are, because there's nothing to screw up if I get it wrong!" He beamed with pride.

"Not bad, Brad. Not bad, at all." I shared his beam. "In fact, when it comes to enemies, competitors and prospective customers, you better assume your butt off. Otherwise you'll have no chance of anticipating their actions. You might as well play in a snow storm with your pants around your ankles."

He shook his head. "Yeh, well, that was entertaining. But I gotta go."

I'm not sure he fully appreciated Minnesota imagery. Sometimes grandpa's clichés were duds. Oh well.

Chapter 5
ASSHOLES

Becky called two days before my next meeting with Brad. "What did you do to him?" She asked. "He came home muttering – 'everybody's an asshole on Thursday... on Thursday ... everybody ... but, but, but ...'".

"But, what?" I asked.
"Me too" said Becky. "I got in his face and said "but, but, but what, Brad?' He stared at me blankly for a second then broke into a big grin. "But some of us are assholes all week long,' he laughed. 'All week ... But most of us aren't'. He hugged me. 'Most of us aren't. I've been missing that point.'"

"Sounds like an epiphany to me." I said.
"More like an epiphany and jelly sandwich," she retorted. "Is he losing it?"

"Sounds more like he's finding it, if you ask me. We've been working through some pretty heavy stuff. Other than the muttering, how has he been?"
"Scary. You know him. Tighter than a drum; like a coiled spring. Not this week. It's like the guy who courted me moved back in. Sweet, helpful, attentive. What the hell is going on?"

"Becky, you're a good wife. And I appreciate your concern, but I have to honor the sanctity of confidentiality."
"Not anymore Doc, 'cause he just incorporated me into his therapy this week."

"Oh, how so?"
"I became his 'Study Buddy'. Did you make this assignment?"

"No, I didn't. What assignment?" Brad had just thrown me a curve ball.
"We spend 55 minutes every night, in intense conversation. No more. No less. In fact, he often ends them by standing and thanking me for coming. It's weird, but exciting too."

"How so?" I asked.
"We've spent the week talking about assholes."

"Hah" I blurted.
"No, seriously. It's been a symposium on the nature of assholedness and what causes people to act thusly. But wait. The most interesting part is that we've also focused on what causes us to see people as assholes."

"And what did you come up with?" I asked.
"Are you at your computer?" she replied.

"Yeh".
"I sent you something before I called. See it?"

"Yeh. I opened the pdf file she'd attached. ... It's a handwritten note from Brad. 'She's in the loop.' He says."
"Well?"

"OK. You're in. To a point. What else have you got?"
"I'm sending it now. We wrote a paper together. 17 pages. I haven't done that since college. It was actually kinda fun."

I was impressed. "Terrific. Gimme the Cliff Note version."

"Okay. Here it is," she said. There are three ways to identify an asshole.
1. His actions
2. His motives
3. His tactics"

"OK," I said. "A little more meat please."

She giggled, "An asshole's actions are destructive --- of individuals, relationships, groups or goals."

"OK, what about the motives?"

"This one was interesting," she said. "It's not so much that they're despicable. But they <u>are</u> always self-centered. An asshole does constant gap analysis, and every action is centered on making sure that he, or she, comes out ahead.

"What about the Tactics?"

"They're despicable. Kneecapping, backstabbing, heaving people under the bus. And always in public. Assholes work out in the open, not in the shadows. At least when they're trying to diminish the other party. The opposite is true when they're trying to build themselves up, though. Then everything is sneaky-sneaky. They're the classic, gold-bricks, gold diggers, cheaters, liars and credit grabbers."

"That's good work. What was your biggest surprise?"

"The practical joke. It is the asshole's favorite weapon. Makes the victim look like a fool, and raises the jokester in other's eyes, because they determine who gets laughed at. And nobody wants to be next. We discovered that practical jokes are actually a form of intimidation, aimed at the audience, not the victim. I never knew that. Heck, I've pulled off my fair share of practical jokes in my day."

"Yeh. I remember some of them. Do they still seem funny now?

"Some, yeh, like the mayonnaise in Melanie's bathing suit," she chuckled, "but most of them, no. They mostly embarrass me now. I hurt people."

"So you were an asshole every Thursday. What about the rest of the week?"

"We asked each other the same question," said Becky. "And we actually took an extended walk down memory lane. No, the rest of the week, every week, we've been consistently nice guys. That was reassuring. Anyway, that's the paper in a nutshell."

"Anything else?" I asked.

"Yeh. I discovered a few things I didn't share with Brad."

"Such as?"

"Such as the meaning of the sexual imagery in all this. Do you know that 92% of people refer to being cheated as getting screwed?"

I shrugged, "Didn't know the exact number, but I'm not surprised."

"I am. I thought getting screwed was supposed to be something positive. Isn't that what men spend their entire adult lives trying to get? I mean really, you'd think they'd speak about it with a bit more reverence."

"Ah, Becky. You miss the point. Screwing *is* very positive to men. *Getting* screwed isn't. It's a question of whether you're the do-er or the do-ee. As a general rule, guys don't like being on the receiving end. If I am, somebody cheated --- hence, I got screwed."

"Ahhh. I see. So explain this; 83% of people refer to the cheater as an asshole. 'Dick' and 'jerk' make up the remaining 17%. Why asshole?"

"Get graphic, Becky. If a guy is going to get screwed, where is that going to occur?"

A momentary pause, then, "Ohhh. I get the connection – but isn't the usage reversed. Shouldn't the victim be referred to as the asshole? I mean, really?"

I chuckled to cover the fact I was blushing. "That's one of the vagaries of human nature. A strange little glitch in human nature. The name game. One kid says, 'You're an asshole.' So the other one fires back, 'No! *You're* the asshole."

"Bear with me here," continued Becky. "The greatest indignity in life is not rape. It's anal rape. Regardless of whether you're male or female, anal rape is the ultimate humiliation."

"Yep. It is the top of the heap when it comes to dominance games."

"So when Brad refers to folks as assholes, he's sending up a red flare, isn't he?"

"Yep. He's announcing that he's firmly in the 1st circle of hell. He's helpless and humiliated."

"Yeh. I'm scared Doc. I think he's heading for a heart attack. Or stroke. His color's not good – kinda splotchy. And when he goes on a rampage…"

"Yeh, his eye bleeds. Have you taken him to the doctor?"

"Every specialist in town. They all give him a clean bill of health. The man has Zen-like qualities, though.

I'll bet his normal blood pressure is over 200 and probably tops 300 when he has one of his temper fits. But when he's at the doctor's --- it's consistently 120/80. Anyway, I've got an appointment at the Mayo Clinic in 3 weeks."

"Good. In the meantime, give him an aspirin a day, and we'll continue whittling away at the source of his temper fits. We're actually making good progress. I think every business owner goes through this kind of stress. Brad's is just different as a matter of degree. I'll keep you posted. Bye."

* * * * * *

Brad walked in chuckling. "How'd you like my little pit bull? I figured I'd sic Becky on you. She'd keep you on your toes."

"She's very impressive. You guys did a lot of work. Where did that come from?"
"I just thought I'd get a jump on things. I knew our topic today would be assholes."

"How?"
"It's the next word in my mantra. 'Why in hell won't these assholes …' Just thought I'd get a head start. So now I know what an asshole is. And I also know that most of my folks are NOT assholes. At least not most of the time. So what's next? The word 'DO'?"

"Not quite so fast. Why do you think you've always been so quick to assume your employees were assholes?"
"Shorthand," said Brad. "I don't have a lot of spare time. I look at actions and infer motivation. Then I act

on the inferred motivation. It saves a lot of time. Yeh, yehyeh. I know what you're gonna say next."

"You do?"
"Yeh. You're gonna pull a Dr. Phil moment --- 'How's that workin' for ya, Brad?'"

"And?"
"It sucks. Turns out I don't give a rip about why people do what they do. We already covered that in our first session, didn't we?"
"Yep"

Different Animals
"Your comment about owners being different animals than employees got me thinking," said Brad. "Maybe their motivations for doing stuff are different than mine would be in the same circumstance. Maybe they're not gold bricking. Maybe they're scared to take a risk. I never stopped to think of it before, but I just might scare the crap out of my employees."

"All over the floor, Brad. You're rich, successful, good looking, 6'2" and you have one hell of a temper. And you have the vocabulary of a longshoreman. I imagine you scare just about everybody that works for you."
"That was never my intent," he shot back.

"Braaaad," I said. "That is always the intent. Fear prevents confrontation. If you keep everyone a tad bit fearful, they're a whole lot less likely to give you pushback on anything you say."
"You ... I ... oh, fuck me." He sat in silence for a moment. ... "I'm such a shit."

"No, you're not a shit. You're just trying to get through the day, and you found a tool that works. But not perfectly. And right now you're on the verge of finding a better tool. And that is always unsettling. Take a break. Breathe."

We sat in silence for a minute or two. A very long time. "Okay," he started, "how do I change this around?"

By this point both of us were sitting on the edge of our seats, elbows on knees, foreheads almost touching. The conversation was in a near whisper, "Go back to what we were talking about last week about being a different animal than your subordinates." I said. "Let's walk through your assumptions about yourself. Are you smart?"

"No. Clever, maybe, but not particularly smart."

"Tell me about clever." I said.

"Clever. You know, um, I can figure out how to solve problems that stump other folks."

"OK. And what's your assumption about the folks that work for you?"

"They could do the same thing, if they tried hard enough."

"Oh? Why is that?"

"Geez, Doc, do I need to spell it out for you?" He stood abruptly and began to pace. "They could do it if they wanted to because they're every bit as smart as I am."

"But you're not smart. You said so yourself."

"Ok. Not smart. Try clever, then. They're every bit as clever as I am."

"Are not."

"What?"

"They aren't. By definition, you're more clever than they are. You just told me that. You're clever because you can figure things out that nobody else can. That eliminates everyone who works for you. They couldn't figure those things out. You could. Ergo ---- "
"Yeh, well…"

"So what kind of a boss gets mad at his employees for not being able to do something that he knows they can't do --- figure things out? "And what kind of a boss puts unrealistic expectations on his employees because he's unwilling to accept his own special gifts?"
"An asshole?"

I let that hang in the air for a while. "Brad, why don't you come back over here and sit?"
"Fuck me" he grunted as he slid dejectedly into his chair. "Just fuck me."

"I have met the enemy…" I intoned,
and Brad finished, "Yeh, and he is I. I know, I know."

More silence.

"The actual term is 'uber-asshole.'" I said. "Literally going above and beyond the actions of a normal asshole. When you own the business you're in position to be an uber-asshole."
"But I never embarrass or humiliate one employee in front of another. Never do practical jokes. Never belittle, berate, knee cap, or heave them under the bus."

"Stop, Brad. I'm going to tell you something very difficult to hear. You behave like a textbook uber-asshole. Not individually. In fact, at that level you're a downright nice guy. But at the collective level, oh my god. You humiliate, degrade and diminish your people every damn day. Every day, Brad. You just do it to them as a group, not as individuals. You sit here in this office every week and essentially repeat your sacred mantra – 'why the hell won't those assholes do what I tell them to do?' As though they are stupid or evil, or both. Week in. Week out. Does it ever occur to you that two of your folks go to church with me? In fact we serve on the church board together. Another of them is my son's scoutmaster. Another is working on a doctorate in neuro-linguistics, and one of them is dating my daughter?"

He was crest-fallen. "I didn't know. I'm so …"

"Brad, every company has two employees on a church board, one in scouting, one working on an advanced degree and one dating someone else's daughter. And a whole lot more, to boot. How can you be so dismissive? They are plugging along, most of them doing the best they can. They simply don't have your special gifts, and they certainly don't feel safe enough to take any risks whatsoever, because they know how you feel about them."

"I have to go," said Brad.

"Not quite yet, Brad. What you've done is a bad thing. But you are a good man."

"Oh come on." He said.

"No. I mean it." I said. "A complete asshole would never get this far. They never acknowledge responsibility. They never accept criticism. They never engage in introspection. Three minutes ago I was telling you things no man wants to hear, and that no asshole would tolerate. You have not taken a swing at me, verbally or physically. You have not pulled a gun or thrown a lamp. Those are all marks of true goodness. So your goodness is not the issue. Your choices are. You're at one of those decision points now. Simple question. Do you want to lead your life a different way?"

"Would that I could," said Brad. "You got another trick in your magic bag?"

"No magic. But a couple of suggestions that might help. The first one comes from Adam Smith, the father of capitalism."

"Back in the 1700s?" asked Brad. "This could be good. What did Adam say?"

I tapped the table for emphasis "Look beyond your peasants."

"That's it?" asked Brad. "What the hell does that mean?"

"The king of England and the King of France had been in a pissing match for a good 200 years. Their relative opulence was a measure of their wealth and therefore told them both who the winner was.

The King of England, however, took his eye off the ball in the mid 1200s because he didn't think he could keep up. Instead of comparing his wealth to the wealth of the king of France he started measuring himself against his own peasants. So anytime one of them got close, the king would confiscate the poor schlep's property, cattle and kids. It kept the peasants at bay, but he fell further and further behind the king of France.

Smith came in and said get your eye back on the prize. Look beyond your peasants. Look at King Louis, over in France. And stop confiscating property from your peasants. Instead, help them all get prosperous and just take a reasonable skim of their income. Do that and you'll bury France with your wealth.

The King of England paid attention. His wealth grew by leaps and bounds, and when the king turned into Queen Victoria, the Empire reached its zenith. God save the queen."

    By this time Brad's eyes were rolling. "What the hell does this have to do with me?"

I leaned toward him. "You spend the bulk or your time and energy obsessing about how your employees are screwing you. Stop fearing your own employees. Instead help them get prosperous. As they do, your cut of the pie will swamp out your competitors. Look beyond your peasants."

    "I … You … you may have a point there." He grinned and leaned back. "What else you got?"

"Be a happy divorcee."

    "Be a happy divorcee…" he mulled a second. "Okay, I'll bite. What's that mean?"

"Do you know what supports the legal profession in America?" I asked. "It's hatred. Blind, gut wrenching hatred, and the accompanying need to cut a pound of flesh off the other party. And you know what fuels hatred? Being trapped in a bad situation. If you could just walk away when a disagreement surfaced, things would be fine.

"It's trying to make a bad relationship work that drives us nuts. So walk away. Only do what comes easy --- and that includes relationships. So hire slow and fire quick. Don't make excuses for new employees. Make your judgments before their probationary period ends.

    "Okay. I'll grant you that one as well. But that doesn't help me much right at the moment. Most of my employees have been with me at least 3 years. And the ones causing the most problems are the one's who've been there over five. What do I do with those assholes?"

"Did I ever tell you about the Transactional Web, Brad?"
"Nope."

"Would you like to hear about it?"
He checked his watch. "Yeh, sure. Tell me about the Web."

I get prickly heat anytime someone is dismissive of me. So I took a moment to tear Brad a new one of those things we were talking about today. That's the great thing about counseling. You gain so many tools for destroying the client if and when you wish to. This was just a shot across the bow, though. No real damage was done.
"I'm sorry," he said. "Yeh, I need to hear this."

"Yeh, you do. The web is made up of all the various issues on which we interact with a person, over all the time periods that we interact. Let's say I supervise Charlie on a daily basis. And we also serve on a quality control council together. That's two issues, and numerous time frames. Right?"
"Yeh. It's like a box and arrow flow chart. I got it."

"Ok. Two things you can do. Spend more time with Charlie on each interaction on both of the issues. Find out about his family. Keep notes. Talk about that during each interaction. Congrats! You just created a third issue for the two of you. Try putting him on a planning committee with you as well. Now you've got 4 issues."
"Why would I do that? Charlie's an asshole."

"Then fire him!" I snapped.

"I can't. He's not *that* much of an asshole," smiled Brad.

"Well then ... you need to increase the number of issues between you two," I said.

"Why?" asked Brad.

"The law of inverses"

"The what?" he asked.

"The Law of inverses. The more complex your relationship with Charlie becomes, the less likely each of you will be an asshole to the other. The Law of Inverses."

He opened his mouth to retort but nothing came out. Instead, his eyes rolled up to the right. "You're right," he said. It worked that way for Mark Henry and me back in 2nd grade. Huh. I haven't thought of Mark in 40 years. Hmmm."

We were a minute over our allotted time. Without being asked, he stood and slowly walked out the door, closing it quietly behind him.

Chapter 6
DO

Brad walked in a bit sheepishly. "I left abruptly last week. Sorry. That was rough."

"Yeh."
"But I made a decision. Knew it before I left. Actually I made it a long time ago. Of course I want to do things differently. That's why I submit myself to these little torturing sessions. Tutoring sessions. I'm sorry. Small difference." He grinned a little.

"I know. It just takes a lot of work to admit things to ourselves openly, doesn't it?"
"Yeh, well at least we know I'm thinking about this stuff. What's next?"

"Ah, what's next? Today is action verb day. We're gonna talk about "DO". What exactly do you want from your folks, Brad?"
"I want them to do what I tell them to do."

"Obedience. OK."
"Not obedience."

No?"
"Well, yeh. But that sounds kinda harsh, don't you think?"

"Are you putting harsh requirements on them? If so, why sugarcoat it? Obedience works for the Marines. It could work for you as well."

"Good point." Said Brad. "Why do you ask?"

"I don't think that's the only thing you want from your folks. Based on what I know of you and some of the other things you've said these past weeks, a lot of your frustration comes from the fact that your folks are not showing initiative."

"None. Nobody seems to see what needs to be done, even when it's staring them in the face. Nothing. I just get blank looks. Drives me nuts."

"I see. But once you point out a problem, everything swings into gear?"

"You'd think. But still, nada. They mill around, but nobody does anything. I have to stop what I'm doing and map out a specific course of action, and give very detailed job assignments to folks."

"And then?"

"And then they do fine. Why the hell couldn't they have done fine on their own?"

"Because you didn't give them permission. Brad, your folks are doing exactly what you trained them to do, which is nothing --- until you tell them exactly what to do. They are being obedient. This is what obedience looks like. You've got exactly what you've been demanding. Your people only do what you specifically tell them to do. And only when you tell them specifically."

"The rest of the time they're just rolling around in neutral, keeping the engine warm."

"Exactly." Two seconds of dead air, just for effect, then, "How's that working for you?"

Brad flushed, "When the gods wish to curse us, they grant us our prayers." He did that little gesture we all do when we've embarrassed ourselves, then looked up. "There's a better way, isn't there?"

"Different." I said. "You get to decide if it's better." I leaned back and put my hands behind my head. How do you give permission, Brad?

He pondered for a bit, then responded, "It depends. If you're giving permission to exercise a freedom, you only have to say it once. Bingo. You've just given permission for all time. Try getting that one back."

I nodded my head and chuckled a bit. Like I said, Brad was one of the best and brightest. Right then he was surprising me with the complexity of his thought.

"But here's the interesting one," Brad continued. "When you're giving permission to take on a responsibility, you have to say it again and again, and write it down, and have pep rallies over it and give out awards for it."

"Why is that?" I asked.

"I dunno," he said. "But gimme a minute. It … I know! Risk. When they take on a responsibility they have no place to hide. If it blows up, I could climb down their throats. Or fire them. They're out there all by themselves."

"Sound like the three circles of Hell, doesn't it?" I asked. "Uncertainty, risk <u>and</u> isolation. That's the trifecta, isn't it? I'm not inviting them to show initiative, I'm consigning them to Hell. Damn … how am I supposed to run a company, then?"

"By pulling initiative out of Hell." *(In case you missed it, the prior two paragraphs might just be the crux of this book)*

"How?"

"I am so glad you asked. It just so happens that I have a few suggestions. Would you like to hear them?"
"Please"

"OK. Give them company, safety and a little certainty. Hang on a second. Let me be my own straight man. How do you do that? Start by telling them exactly what you need --- in general terms. Our policy and procedures simply can't anticipate every contingent in life. When you see a problem, I need, want and expect you to fix it, clean up after it or help others recover from it, whichever is most pressing.

If there is time, contact me, tell me what the problem is and what your suggestion is for fixing it. I promise that I will respond by asking you what you need. When you tell me, then I'll make any final suggestions and give you a green light to address the issue, or we'll assign it to someone else if a specific talent is needed."

"And if there isn't time?" Brad prodded me.

"Then I give them permission to handle things on the spot, and send me an email explaining what happened, what they did and why. And I have to promise that my response will always be 'THANK YOU'. Now what did we learn so that we can prevent this or fix it even better the next time?"… These steps don't eliminate uncertainty, but they do suck a lot of it out of the situation, and that limits risk. So does my promise of safety. Notice that I assure them again and again that my response to them will be positive. And I give them the best company in the whole firm. Me. The boss. You can't buy better company than that. We're in it together." I took a breath. "How's that compare with what you do?"

"Well," said Brad, "except for the promises, the green lights and the consultation stuff I'd say it's identical." He started a sick self-loathing laugh.

I fiddled with something for a second or two, can't remember what, just to give him a chance to recover, "Look, you just need to use the right tool in the right location. At the macro level, you've got to be a tyrant. If our primary target is housewives with a lisp, then nail the sucker who's spending time and money chasing down single truck drivers. And if our chief selling point is speedy service, crucify anyone who slows down the process. You absolutely have to have alignment when it comes to the basics of vision, values and goals. Be clear. Be consistent. Be ruthless in enforcing them. That's the macro level.

You get that straight and you can be as loose as a goose on the micro stuff. Don't sweat whether they use their left hand or their right. It's not important. Let it go. In fact – go one step further. Encourage them to discover a hands-free way to do the task in question; or to figure a way to eliminate that task altogether.

"Doc. I am _so_ bad at this."

"Not bad, Grasshopper. Just incomplete. Permission is like dew. It evaporates at the first sign of heat."

He gave me a "you've got to be kidding" look.

"I saw the Dali Llama once" I shrugged. "I've been waiting 20 years to use that line." We both laughed. "Let's focus things here a bit better, now. What is it you're trying to influence here? Behavior has two parts: thinking and doing. Which are you trying to control?"

"Is there a right answer here?" asked Brad, "because it feels like a trick question." I shook my head. "The way our conversation has been going I'd say I should focus on controlling thoughts and let folks' actions grow naturally from them. But I'd have to disagree with myself. Too cumbersome, too complex. I've proven I lack the skill to discover what folks think, so I'll just focus on what I can see, which is their behavior. ----- how'd I do?"

"Brad. You re 48 years old. You make more money than God. Why do you care how well I think you did?"

" I just do. How'd I do?"

"You did surprisingly well. Both in terms of your line of thought and in terms of your final decision. Bravo." He grinned. "Now," I continued, "where do you exercise this influence? In their private realm or strictly in your business realm?"

"Old man, you can not trip me up on this. I read your book. I know you can't separate the personal from the professional." He grinned again. "I gotcha."

"By the toe, maybe," I said, "They're mixed together, but still fairly distinct. Stop dodging the question."

"If I were a Libertarian, I wouldn't do either. It's nobody's business what I think or do." He sucked on his teeth for a minute.

"If I were a Democrat, I'd demand blind adherence to the proper thoughts, but I'd forgive everyone for screwing up the actions part." Deep in thought for a moment.

"And if I were a Republican, I'd demand the whole shebang: blind adherence to the proper thoughts, lock step obedience on proper actions, and I'd sic Ann Coulter on anyone who got out of line."

He had me. He was good. I chuckled "Not bad at all. The big decision here is whether to run your company with rules or boundaries. Rules say do (or think) this, then this, then this etc. Boundaries say, I'd like you to think (or work) on this for awhile but don't spend more than 8 hours and $52,000 on it. Let me know what you come up with. What do you think?"

Brad pondered a moment, "I think I've been running everything by rules. And I think I'd like to change that a bit. I'd like to have my folks think for me, so I'll try using boundaries when it comes to what they think."

"And when it comes to what they do..?"

"When it comes to what they do ... I'm gonna stick with rules for a while. Baby steps, Doc. Baby steps. Together, maybe me and my folks will get to boundaries on the actions as well."

"I can live with that," I said. "OK, last question for today. Do you focus on what, or how?"

"Explain," Brad said.

"When we focus on What, we're focusing on what gets accomplished – the outcomes. Did market share go up? By how much? At what level of profit? That type of thing.

"When we focus on how, we focus on how we do the minutia of the business – the inputs. How many hours, and how many dollars did we spend on one task or another? Who got to call the shots? Who got left doing the grunt work? That type of thing." I scratched my nose to give him time to anticipate my next question.

"Inputs. The How. That's what we've been focusing on. I'm sick of it. It's created a culture of subcontractors, with everyone starting every conversation with "That's not my area". That goes back to the three circles of Hell doesn't it? Everyone trying to avoid risk, and hide in the crowd. My fault, I know.
 "But if it's my bad, then it can also be my good. I can fix this, can't I? It's part of … it's like, like Jacob's ladder. In the Bible the stairway to heaven. We inject some safety, give folks permission, and focus on outcomes, and up we go – out of Hell and into Heaven. I'm babbling aren't I?"

"Yes, you are" I laughed. "But it's good babble. It is, most assuredly, good babble."
 He rose to leave and as we shook hands I asked him to ponder one question for the week. "Which actions are best driven by command, and which by massage?"

Chapter 7
LOVE IS A VERB

Brad rolled into my office in what can only be called an ebullient mood - like somebody had just shaken a bottle of coke and was spraying the room. "Honest to God Doc, it is the greatest thing since sliced bread. Becky turned me on to it. It's so easy it feels like a gimmick. You know this. I know you know. I didn't know it, though. And you knew that. Well, or course you did. How did you know that I didn't know? Did you know? You did, didn't you? Probably so. Looking back, it's obvious I didn't know. You know what I mean?" He stood there grinning like a Cheshire cat, panting. "You know?"

I laughed. "Sorry, Brad. I'm not very facile with Babble. Could you translate for me? Use small words and take a breath now and then. What is it that Becky and I know but you didn't know until this past week?"

He pulled his chair closer to mine and sat so that our knees were almost touching. "The secret of the universe. The four words that change everything; 'Love is a verb.'" Again with the grin.

I pushed my chair back and stood up. "OK. Pull your chair to where mine was" I said. He did so. Then I moved my chair to where his used to sit. "Nonono no," I commanded. "Don't turn around. We're going to try an experiment. I'm gonna sit back here and stare at the back of your head. You just sit there with your eyes closed while we have the following conversation."

"This is very weird, Doc."

"Yeh. Well so are you at the moment." He chortled at this, but I continued, "Right now your brain is having an electric storm. You're so excited that every synapse is firing at once. I'm surprised you're able to talk and walk at the same time."

"God, you're right. It's like a bottle of champagne up there, just fizzing away."

"OK. So let's reel it back in a bit so we can walk our way through this. Let's start with 30 seconds of silence. Close your eyes. Inhale slow, exhale to the count of 7. Good, just keep repeating that. Good."

I will confess that I was pulling stuff out of my jockey shorts on this. I just needed to get him out of my face and space, and this rigmarole was the only ego-protective idea I had on the spur of the moment. "OK." I continued. "Keep your eyes closed. Now go back to 'Love is a verb.' Tell me what that means."

"That means it ain't a state of being." I couldn't tell whether he had his eyes closed or not, but he was talking with his hands and shoulders, so I assumed he did. "A state of being is static. Internal, Quiet. Dry. A verb is interactive. I do something to something, or someone ... and since every action has an equal and opposite reaction, I'll get something back in return. You see?"

"Not quite" I said. "Tell me a bit more."

"Look. Love is not what we feel. It's what we do." He heard my prep breath. "Not yet. Let me finish. I'm not denying that we feel something inside when we love. I'm saying that our feelings are a by-product of love; they're not the love itself. You see?"

"OK. So where does this insight take you?"

"Are you really this dense," he asked, "or are you just playing the fool to make a point?"

"Let's assume I'm just playing the fool," I said. "Humor me."

"OK" he sighed and settled deeper into his chair. "Where does this take us? OK. I've been assuming that my folks were out to screw me. That presupposes a negative attitude on their part, which we can assume grew out of negative feelings about me. It's like the great looking babe in school who won't give you the time of day. In fact, she disses you whenever you try to make a move."

"Disses?"

"Yeh. 'Diss'. Dismisses. She dismisses you whenever you make a move."

"Ahhhh"

"OK. It's like that. So how do you change that?"

"Send her flowers. Buy her jewelry. Write her love songs. Rent a billboard."

"Geeze Doc. How'd you ever get laid? One of those might be a good icebreaker. But it takes more than that. You've got to ... well ... you've got to buy her chairs."

"What???" He had me with this one. "What the heck does that mean? Buy her chairs."

"It's from an old John Travolta movie. He's got a crush on this woman who hand makes these really ugly and uncomfortable chairs out of tree limbs. She won't give him the time of day. So he offers to sell her chairs out of his gas station. The chairs start to move. She makes a little money. And their relationship takes off from there. Turns out no one ever bought her chairs. John would just store them in his barn one at a time and give her money for each one he stashed. He loved her by buying her chairs, even though they were ugly and uncomfortable. That's how you change folks' feelings. You buy their chairs. Love is a verb."

"Brad. That's brilliant! No. Don't turn around. That is actually a great tactic for courting a woman. But getting into a girl's pants is a far cry from managing the motivations of your factory personnel."

"Not as far as you think," he chuckled. "Look. Love is a verb. It's a verb. Think about that. What do you <u>do</u> when you're in love? It's a finite set. Not hard. When you're in love:
- ➢ "You always have time for her. You turn off your phone, TV or video game. Turn your back on your computer, and never – ever – continue working while she's trying to talk to you. Because you are enthralled by her.
- ➢ "You focus on her 100% when she talks. You lean toward her, your breathing matches hers. Your pupils dilate. You listen to her words and her intent. You respond to what she has said. And you wait your turn, because what she says has merit.
- ➢ "You take the initiative in contacting her. And you let her know that's because she's important to you.
- ➢ "You take the initiative in pleasing her, too. You give her gifts and compliments. You rub her back and feet. You draw a bath for her. You fondle her thoroughly and completely, at least once a day. And you have sex with her the way <u>she</u> wants to have it.
- ➢ "You are her champion with others. You protect her from threats large and small. You advocate for

her, you occasionally explain her to others. You smooth her path whenever possible. And you never throw her under the bus.

> "And you honor her by a ready dependence on three crucial phrases

   1. "That's an excellent point. I've changed my mind,
   2. "I am so sorry. I was wrong. How can I make this right?
   3. "That was wonderful. Thank you so much."

I let the last points hang in the air for a bit, then asked Brad to open his eyes and turn his chair around so we were looking at each other. "Exceptional rendition, Brad. You've updated things a bit. But you're in line with the pros. I first encountered this approach in the discourses of Cicero. It's also the core of How to Win Friends and Influence People the perennial best seller by Dale Carnegie. It shows up in Men are from Mars and Women are from Venus. And, most recently, I read it in a book on servant leadership that we're reading for my church council. What you've discovered is the core of what has come to be called the Emotional Intelligence movement."

"You son of a bitch!" he belly laughed. "You knew this stuff all along. You son of a bitch. That was good. But here's the thing. Becky and I never read any of that stuff about influencing Martian women or influencing Cicero. Honest. So where'd that come from?"

I smiled. "Emotional Intelligence. That's where it came from. Your innate emotional intelligence. I think we're born with it. It's like our innate understanding of pain and pleasure, good and bad, right and wrong. You're just a bit more articulate than the average guy, so you packaged it well."

"Cool. Here's the thing. It transfers from the bedroom to the boardroom, and to the factory floor. Not directly. You substitute for the sex and touching stuff. But everything else transfers as is. Turns out that I've been ignoring my key reports for years. They walk in and I never look up. I just give 'em the barrel roll hand signal and half listen, all without losing a beat in my texting, emailing, web searching or monitoring stock prices. Oh I talk to them a lot, and I require them to talk to me a lot – at least once a week – to see if they hit their numbers for that week. But it's been a long time since I really asked anyone for their opinion. And even longer since I actually listened to what they thought. I know. I know. Fuck me."

I just held out my hands and cocked my head.
He continued, "Well, I used it this week. Love is a verb. It was pretty impressive. Snarley looks disappeared. Posture improved. Defensive actions lightened up. It was like I'd opened the window shades."

"Did you look in the mirror?" I asked.
"No, I ... No. Do I look different?"

I chuckled, "Yeh. Your posture's better. So's your voice. And someone loosened that bolt in the middle of your forehead. The one that pulls all the furrows in your brow toward the top of your nose. You see, it's tough to be snarley when you're in mid-seduction."

"So ... maybe they were just reacting to ME being more positive?"

"Ladies and gentlemen. Learning has just occurred." I beamed at him.

"Son of a bitch." He murmured. "So that's all it takes?"

"No. But it sure creates a great context for all the other stuff, doesn't it?"

"Yeh. But one of the guys told me I was pursuing a pussy strategy. I didn't appreciate that."

"Why not?"

"It only looks like I'm being a pussy. It's just basic human decency."

"Are you sure that's what he meant? Maybe he went to State University."

"Yeh, he did. What's that got to do with it?"

"Did he major in Psych?"

"Yeh"

"Then he meant something different. He studied under old Fletcher Smyth, who had studied under Freud, or Viktor Frankl or Carl Jung. I forget which. Anyway, Smyth was famous for telling his teaching assistants about the 'Pussy Strategy' that Freud or whoever had taught him. It was just the standard emotional intelligence stuff."

"So why'd he call it the 'Pussy Strategy'?"

Because his mentor had told him that with this strategy you could get all the pussy you wanted. Hence – 'Pussy Strategy'."

Quick giggle. "He's right. Bless his heart. It does work." He sat there chuckling quietly for a moment while he rubbed his hands. "And I know why it works." He said. "It makes them visible. I see them. It tells them I see them. Like in the movie <u>Avatar.</u> 'I see you' means I see your heart, your soul, your mind – all together. It's like the Old Testament term – Abraham 'knew' Sarah. It wasn't a euphemism for sex. It was a statement that sex was much more than friction. You knew the girl down to the very fiber of your being."

"OK. So it makes them visible. And that triggers what?"
"Wait." he showed me his palm. "Wait. We did this last week or the week before. The light bulb factory. The Hawthorne effect. Making them visible triggers the Hawthorne Effect. It changes their behavior."

"Ah, Grasshopper. You make me proud."
He grinned. "Fuck me. Here's my theory. Visibility kills their sense of isolation. And the fact that I listen gives them reason to believe that they are not helpless, since I may act on what they say. And when helplessness recedes, so does hopelessness. And that relieves stress and eventually anxiety. And all of that pulls them out of one of the circles of Hell."

"Not bad for a day's work." I said. "What you're doing is building your psychic bank account with them. They're the bank. Every time you convince them you like them, a deposit is made. Every time you exhibit trust, clink! Another deposit. Every time you listen. Every time you let them be a star, help them achieve a goal, serve as their ambassador and buffer – clink, clink clink. You build your psychic nest egg. Then when you need it – they dole out the treasure, which they now owe you. He nodded.

"But there's a catch." I said. "You have to do this all the time, now. Remember that part of about fondling her, every day? Well that's what you need to do. Psychic fondling. Every day. Constantly let them know they're visible and appreciated."

"Every day?"

"Yep. Every day. You ever seen a couple that was once young and in love, after the juice is gone?"

"Yeh. I think my own folks were just such a couple. Cordial, but dry. They must have been extremely lonely together. But my Uncle Harry still has a love affair with Aunt Sally. And they're a lot older than my folks were. He gooses her a lot. And she giggles every damn time."

"They're still fondling, physically as well as emotionally. It keeps the juice flowing."

"Why is that?"

"Because it is so easy to slip back into invisibility and the parade of horribles that follows it. We are so willing to believe the worst, or least, about ourselves. And the world seems so eager to help us do so. If we don't have someone whispering in our ear how wonderful we are, we just let the world suck away the juice."

"Becky says we have to hear a compliment 5 times before we believe it. But we only need to hear a criticism once."

"Becky's a bright girl."

Chapter 8
UNREQUITED LOVE

Brad was crestfallen. "I give up Doc. I spent the whole week loving those turkeys like a verb. I listened. I paused. I focused. I stroked. I took the time to explain. So ask me what happened."

"I'll bite. What happened?"
"Shit happened, that's what. Everyone stopped working. Started yelling at me. Bitching and moaning about everything. Skipping work. Taking advantage, dogging it, faking injuries. Milking Worker's Comp. I can't deal with this crap." He buried his head in his hands.

At times like this, I play the name game. 'Who? Gimme his name." It quickly cuts "everyone" down to "a couple of guys". It's a way to bring perspective and scale into a crisis situation. The upshot was that some bad things had happened in response to his love as a verb offensive. One guy filed a Worker's Comp claim that was clearly ludicrous. Four employees skipped work for two days (and were spotted at the bowling alley). Two of his black female employees pulled that "sassy in your face ghetto bitch" routine on him. Hand signals and everything. They were so enraged by life in general, that Brad couldn't quite recall why, exactly, they were angry with him. Later in the day two other employees apologized for the Ladies as much as possible without throwing them under the bus. It turns out that Brad had problems with 7 of his employees, not all 163. Everyone else had fluctuated between a mildly pleasant reaction and complete indifference. But productivity did decline by 4% last week, which was not all accounted for by the time lost to the all hands meetings, walk-about conversations and bowling gigs. Something was amiss. Just not quite as big as Brad's initial assessment.

"So why do you think you had these problems, this week?" I asked.
"Because I looked like a pussy."

"That depends. How did you react to these indiscretions?"
"I didn't. I haven't. I couldn't. I'm the 'love doctor'. How do I turn around and drop a hammer on folks without negating that? You put me between a rock and a hard place, Doc."

"Brad. Do you love your kids?"
"Yeh."

"Did you ever spank them?"
"Yeh."

"Did the love stop?"
"Yeh. But only for a little while."

"So tell me again why discipline has to break down in the midst of a love offensive."
He grinned sheepishly. "It doesn't. Okay. I got it. What do you suggest?"

"Proportional Response. It works in international relationships. It might work in micro relationships as well."
"Okay. I got it. Here's what I do. If or when the doctor denies the Worker's Comp claim, I will immediately fire that little turd. That's an honor

violation. The bowling buddies lose two days pay, plus an extra two days pay for failing to properly notify their supervisor of their requests for a personal day."

"That's good," I chuckled. "That plays right to the policy book. And what will you do with your sisters of color?"

"Sisters of color? Well, first and foremost, I can't ignore the fact that they're black. And I can't ignore the fact that their behavior was inappropriate. It was disruptive and rude. It hijacked the agenda for the rest of the meeting. It was emotionally and physically threatening. And, ultimately, it was racist. The problem is, they didn't break any company policies."

"So what are you going to do?" I asked.
"I'm not sure."

"What would you do if one of your kids started acting like a bully?"

"Good point. Lemme think. If … in that case my obligation is to safeguard the other kids and family members. I'd isolate the bully and snuff the behavior."

"You can't snuff an employee, Brad."

"That is a silly rule. Seriously – they're gonna snuff themselves. Here's what I'm going to do. I'll call each one in individually and explain to them that their behavior has a chilling effect on the other employees that is intolerable. Therefore I have three options. I'll explain the options and let each one pick their own solution.

Option 1 – She keeps here job, *if* she writes an apology to the employees that meets my approval, which I post on every bulletin board in the place. In addition, she is fined a day's pay and is put on probation for 90 days.

Any further evidence of anger management issues and she is fired on the spot. These conditions also to be posted on every bulletin board.

Option 2 – She is fired summarily. And I post the reason why on every bulletin board.

"Is that all?"

He crossed the room in two strides. "All? Hell no, that's not all. We have a god damned black president now. Do you realize that? And I still pay my taxes. So does every other white guy in America. I haven't moved to New Zealand. I haven't bought a gun. I've accepted the son of a bitch. Hell, I even came close to voting for him. So this shit ends today. It's time for the blacks to man-up. I declare discrimination to be over. It's over. Do you fucking understand me? Over! I am not a racist. I am not a white devil. And I will be boiled in fucking oil before I let one more black bastard even hint that I am." And having exhausted his rage he stood there not knowing what to do. So he stuck his hands in his pants and walked to the window.

Silence did its slow roll across the space between us.
"I see."

No response.

"I'm not sure you fully grasp the concept of proportional response, Brad."

He turned and showed eyes brimming with tears. "No, Doc. It's you who doesn't understand proportional response. I've got a workforce that smells like low hanging fruit. If I were a union organizer I'd be sniffing around the back door. My company is fighting for survival. And as a straight white entrepreneur I'm under constant attack: from blacks, from enviro-nazis, from angry women, and anyone else with a politically correct axe to grind. I'm just trying to do something with my life here. I don't deserve the shit I get."

"No, you don't." He was right. I knew that as well as you. But I also knew that he was suffering a dangerous case of the 'poor me's'. "I can't solve the racial tensions, Brad. They're too deeply imbedded. And you may be right about the union. You've put your folks under a lot of pressure for a lot of years, without a lot of love. So you might be right." I went back to my chair, hoping he'd do the same. "Look, we never have control over the past. And stressing over the future is an exercise in futility. First, speculative suffering never buys off the gods of war. Second, the future never turns out the way we expect it to, anyway. All we have is today. Make changes, today. Love folks, today. Be fair to them, today. Demand that they do the same, today."

"That's what I'm saying. Doc. That's exactly what I'm saying."

"You know this will ignite a firestorm. But I'll tell you what, my friend. I think you should do it. Just the way you've planned." He gave me a surprised look as he sat down.
"No strings? No buts?" He wasn't quite sure what my agenda was.

"Look Brad. You've built a successful firm based in large measure on your entrepreneurial gut. I say obey it here, as well. Just check with your lawyer first."
"To see if I can do it?"

"No. You're gonna do it. That's your decision, not his. You're gonna do it. What you want to talk to him about is the next step. The shit storm that follows. Civil rights.

Women's rights. Union rights. Probably gay rights and the greenies as well, just for good measure. Simply participating in the shit storm gives them all a marvelous anchor for this year's fund raising."

"You think... ?"

"Oh, hell yes. It'll be a cage fight.
"So, what do you think I should do?"

"Me. I'd fire those angry bitches outright and I'd post that very eloquent statement you just unleashed on me – including the stuff about Obama. That was actually insightful and heart felt. I would also restate your commitment to your love offensive and state that part of it is mutual respect, which only lives within civil discourse. And I would go on to define what civil discourse is. Give 'em the rules of decorum you demand. Pledge to honor them yourself. And offer the door to anyone unable to comply. Make it clear, simple and fair."

He did a little air boxing.

"How do you feel?"
"Pumped."

"Why is that?"
"Cause I'm no longer the doormat."

"Because you just stepped out of the first circle of hell. You decided to not be helpless anymore. Congratulations, Brad. You just bought a gun."
He grinned from ear to ear for a minute. "Yeh, I did. I most certainly bought myself a gun. Am I gonna survive this?"

"I honestly don't know, Brad. But I know for a fact that you weren't going to survive the way you were going. You were abusing your people, neglecting them and distrusting them at every turn. When you stop seeing yourself as a helpless victim, you'll actually start treating your people better. With the added benefit that you'll treat yourself better as well. Are we good?"

He hopped out or his chair and I mirrored him. "We're good. Hell, we're great!" We high-fived then down-lowed, then gleefully performed a full array of swats and hand signals from our youth. We collapsed back into our chairs amidst the gales of laughter that follow a last minute hail-Mary pass that succeeds.

I finally leaned forward. "You know. There's only one way in hell this has any chance to succeed."

He mirrored. "What's that?"

"You've got to take the ego out of this. Your reaction today has been that of a jilted lover. You bathed them in love for a full week; you did all the things that should have triggered a like response from them. But instead of a groundswell of affection, you were met with indifference at best and outright attack at worst. They didn't shift from fear to love. At best, they simply shifted from fear to *not* fear. So you reacted as any jilted lover does. You started heaving clothes out the window."

"Too much?"

"By a hair. Love takes time, Brad. They have to learn what it feels like, and they need to trust that you will reciprocate to the affection they give you."

"But it felt good."

"You bet. It always feels good to step out of hell, even for a moment."

"Are you saying I need to step back into hell?"

"Oh geeze no. Everything you said, needs to be said. Everything you want to do, needs to be done. I'm just saying you need to squeeze your ego out of the picture, first. Forget getting your feelings hurt. Your job is to build a healthy, self-sustaining organization. One that you can walk away from for a month at a time. Otherwise you can never sell it. Then it's just a job. It's not an asset. And you're trapped for life. You tired of being trapped?"

"Oh yeh.

"Okay. Make all this a functional issue. Not a moral issue. You fire the black girls, but not because they're black. And not because no one has the right to talk to you like that. You fire them because that kind of behavior intimidates their fellow workers and harms the open civil discourse necessary to life in an organization. You post your two fisted policy on civil discourse, but not as a chest thumping declaration of your alpha-manliness. You post it as a straightforward statement from the guy who has the authority and responsibility to determine such things.

"Then you fire the little weasel playing his Worker's Comp game. But not because he thought he could outsmart you. You fire him because any breech of honor is intolerable in this organization. It cheapens us all, and contributes to an atmosphere of distrust. You name names. You render judgments. You move on.

"The message you give is this. I love you all, and trust you with my most precious possession, my company. You are to be my faithful stewards, growing each other and my wealth in a manner that allows us all to prosper. When you do that I will joyfully reward you. But if you prove that my trust in you is misplaced, I will isolate you and publicly render you helpless. I will cast you into the first circle of hell. That is my responsibility to the honorable ones, and I take it very seriously."

"Wow!"

"Yeh. Wow. Love is not weak. That's why it gets the pussy."

He laughed all the way out the door.

Chapter 9
WHAT

"I got lots of issues today." He started abruptly. "No small talk. Nothing about Becky and the kids. No sports, politics or anything. Just straight to the "I got lots of issues today".

"Shoot."

"I spent the first two days squeezing my ego out of the situation." He twisted his head to de-kink his neck. "That isn't as easy as you'd think. But I finally got to a point where I felt I was dispassionate. So I fired the angry babes, fined the bowling guys and threw the book at my Worker's Comp guy. Charged him with criminal fraud and fired him the moment the doctor gave me his report. Had an all hands meeting. Talked about my commitment to them and the firm. Explained the rules of civil discourse we were going to follow. Talked about honoring each other. Told them of my responsibility to make sure we had an atmosphere of comity and hope. Then I announced my various disciplinary actions, named names and gave them the reasons why."

"And...?"

"And? The firings were cathartic. One of the ladies threw an absolute fit, throwing things all over the place and screaming at the top of her lungs. She called me every name in the book and was screaming threats as the cops hauled her out. The other one wilted into a pool of tears when her turn came. Weeping and gnashing her teeth. I fully expected her to launch into her "Please don't go firin' me now massa Brad" routine. At least the first one was a consistent bully.

"The Worker's Comp scammer got the perp walk treatment from the cops. Walked him the full length of the factory floor in cuffs. So by the time I got to the bowling guys they were delighted to keep their jobs. They virtually thanked me for the fines."

"And ...?"
"And, reactions were mixed. Folks seemed to appreciate losing the two ladies. A couple of folks said thanks and two asked me what took so long. The rest simply said nothing. No one has said a thing about the scammer. The perp walk traumatized everyone. I did have several folks tell me the bowling fines were great, and one told me they had all been wondering what the point of integrity was around here. Apparently I've been a long time victim of pilfering and malingering. I've had two guys volunteer to help me clean up that mess."

"And ... ?"
"And I had perfect attendance at the all hands meeting. It was tense, and surly and I wasn't sure I was going to make it through. But they warmed up a bit as I spoke about honor and mutual respect. I'm not sure I won a lot of converts, but I didn't face open rebellion. So I count that a win."

"Good. You did an incredibly hard thing. Good for you. So?"
"So --- And ---? What? If you want something, use your words."

I laughed. " Yeh, Okay. My words. You're running a business, Brad. Not a church. Being nice to one another only counts if it translates into profits. So did it?"

"No. Not a dime. I know it's too early to tell for sure. But I don't see any improvement at all. Folks are still milling around waiting for someone else to make their decisions. They still flood me with inane questions. Well, they didn't for a full day after the blood bath. Then they've been making up for lost time ever since."

"So, love doesn't translate into productivity then, does it?"

"No. Why is that?"

"Well, first of all they don't trust you yet. You spent a whole lot of years abusing them, usually by neglect. They're not sure if this change is dependable. That'll take a while, especially since you've got a union organizer or two buying these guys a beer after work just to help them not trust you."

"I've got unions sniffing here?"

"Of course you do."

"Son of a bitch. How do you know that?"

"You told me. Last week. By the time an owner suspects he's got unions at his door, they've been there for a while. You've got unions at the door, Brad."

"Shit."

"Flush. Let's move on. We were talking about why love doesn't translate into productivity. Second reason, fatigue. Stress and fear are tiring. Most people need to sit and rest after a trauma ends. Your folks are resting."

"So being nice to them is bad business for me?"

"In the immediate term, yeh. But that problem will heal itself. Your big problem remains number 3."

"Number three. Oh yeh I agree whole-heartedly. What the hell is number 3?"

"They don't know where the end zone is. Or how they're going to get there."

"Bullshit. I tell them everyday."

"No, you don't, Brad. You tell them how to do the minutia of their jobs everyday. You guys are so busy trying to make a first down that none of you has a clue where the end zone is."

He bristled at that. "I've spent a lifetime putting together processes and procedures. If everyone just did as they were told we'd hit the end zone every single play."

"Yeh, and the second coming will occur at the precise moment that every Jew hits his knees in prayer. But both are impossibilities … because humans are involved. They never do exactly what they're told. Ever."

"Which is why I have to watch them like a hawk."

"You're trying to teach a pig to sing, Brad. It'll never learn. So you just irritate the pig, and wear yourself out in the process."

"Amen to that."

"So how's that working for ya?"

He glared at me out of the top of his eyes, "How dya think?"

"You might want to try approximate control. Show 'em the end zone. Show 'em out of bounds. Tell 'em to score. Bring 'em lots of water and lead the cheering."

"I got lost in the metaphor, Doc. Try it again."

"OK, fair enough. Performance is a direct result of our behavior, right?"

"OK."

"And our behavior is a direct result of our beliefs. Right?" He hesitated. "Come on, Brad. I believe I will hit the ball if I take a swing. So I take a swing."

"In football?"

"In baseball, Brad. Keep up. It's baseball."

"There's an end zone in baseball?"

"That's football. There is no fucking end zone in baseball."

He started to laugh, "There's no crying in baseball, Doc. Try to keep up."

Mixing metaphors in conversation is no more successful than in writing. "Let's go back to the beginning." I drew on my white board while I talked. "Would you agree with me that what you believe, affects how you behave?" He nodded. "And would you agree that what we do, how we behave, affects our performance?" He nodded again.

BELIEFS
⬇
BEhAViOrs
⬇
Performance

"So if I want to affect the behavior that affects performance, what should I do?"

He hesitated, "Work on the beliefs?"

"Yes! But why?" I asked. He hesitated, so I took it, "Because once I affect their beliefs, all their imperfect, incomplete, partially competent actions will at least be aimed in the right direction. It's called 'Alignment'. Why else?"

He kicked into gear, "Efficiency. Because in the time it takes to micro-manage one guy on one task on one machine – or one supervisor, who micro-manages one guy on one task on one machine – in that same amount of time, I could establish a new belief that would redirect the behavior of all 163 of my employees."

I smiled.

"But wait," he intoned with a smirk. "There's more. As the CEO, I'm supposed to float at 30,000 feet looking at the big picture and spotting new rivers of cash. If I'm trying to fiddle with specific behaviors and performance levels, I'm not at 30,000 feet. I'm at 15 feet, or ground level. So – hold on to your hat Doc. I need to work on my own beliefs about what *I* need to be doing."

I nodded.

He grabbed the marker from me and stepped to the board. "So we've been ignoring beliefs, and plowing all our resources into training and processes down here at the behavioral level. And just to make sure we never smell the air at 30,000 feet we use a boundless system of reports and sanctions to tie us down here at the performance level."

I nodded again.

He continued, "How come nobody tells us this stuff?"

"They've been trying," I said, "Since Socrates' time. Your folks need to believe that they're a team. They need to believe that they can win. They need to believe that it matters whether they win. They need to believe that an end zone exists and they need to believe they can get there."

"OK," he responded "But all I've got now is a motivated, but disorganized mob roaming their way in the general direction of the end zone. Tough to make progress."

"Right. So now you put some time and resources into training and processes. Who's a running back? Who's a lineman? What does each one do? How do they coordinate their activities? And you practice. Lord, you practice. This stuff is right out of role theory. Clarity, congruence and consistency."

"But then the game starts and all hell breaks loose, because the other team does new stuff and my guys forget their stuff. So I have to climb back into the trenches and beat them into shape."

"And that's where you go wrong, every single time. What you have to do is let go. Trust your folks. Of course they will screw up specific things now and then. But trust that they will operate as a cooperative team, headed generally in the right direction. Your team does NOT need you down in the trenches. They need you floating up there at 30,000 feet, figuring out how to counteract the new stuff your opponent is doing. So, let go and let yourself float, Brad." I erased the board. "Sit down."

He sat. "Okay, I'm floating. Now when do we talk about the What? What it is I want them to do. That's the next topic in our litany of topics. We got sidetracked for two weeks on love, and we've wasted most of today talking about religion. When do we get to the What?"

"You are *the* dumbest smart guy I think I've ever met. We've been talking about "What" the whole time.
- You treat your employees with affection -- that's ***what***
- You create an atmosphere of safety – that's ***what.***
- You demand civility and honor – that's ***what.***
- You focus on the end zone & how to get there – that's ***what***.
- You stay out of the trenches – that's ***what***.
- You trust your employees – that's ***what***.

Now, do you want more "***what***?". Teach them what is moral, ethical and ennobling. Teach them what is just. Teach them their own potential and the importance of brushing their teeth."

He sat in stunned silence.

I continued. "You wanted me to tell you how to crush the human spirit and force it into compliance. That's the "What" your initial wail was all about. Problem is that traps you into being the jailer. You can never take a vacation when you're a jailer. The moment you step away, the prisoners will rebel and escape and go on a rampage and rape your wife and kill your children. Hell of a life, Brad. Hell of a life."

He shuffled his feet. "Yeh, well …"

I climbed off my soapbox. "Okay, I'm off the soap box."
"Good. It was getting a little sudsy in here."

"Yeh, well, here's an idea for your big 'what'. Teach them to play."
"What?"

"Teach them to play. Here's what I mean. Your son is 12. Is he ever too tired to take out the garbage or rake the leaves?"
"Always."

"Is he ever too tired to play with his friends?"
"Never."

"Why is that?"
"Because work wears you out, and play energizes you."
He started to smile. "Whoa. If we made work into play, my folks would be energized and their performance would take care of itself."

"Over-simplified, but yeah."
"Okay. How do I do it?"

"Start by realizing that play is a fantasy world in which we give expression to our hopes, dreams, fears, wants and needs. And that's true whether we're playing baseball, poker or house.

"It is a separate reality where actions do not denote what they would if performed during "normal reality". The justice department doesn't nail you with an anti-trust suit for the avarice you display playing "Monopoly". And you can literally beat somebody into submission on the football field and get cheered rather than jailed.

"So play is a safe harbor for the soul. As a result, we invest ourselves more fully in play than any other activity known to man. More effort. More focus. More sacrifice. More creativity. More enthusiasm. More desire. More competitiveness." He had moved to the edge of his seat. "You want some of this?" I asked.

"Ye-ah."

"Then all you need to do is supply safety and stimulation."
"Bullshit. Nothing is that simple"

"You're right. There are components. First of all, play is episodic. It has boundaries of time and space. It ends. And then you get to start all over again with a clean slate. Poker is the best example. You get your butt kicked in one hand. So what? They're already re-dealing. Hot dog! Hope springs eternal. Let's play.
"Yeh," snorted Brad, "but work never ends. It is eternal, and all pervasive. How do you get past that one?"

"Nothing is perfect Brad. We can't get rid of those facts. So work can never be pure play. But, it can be made more play-like. Break things into bite-sized chunks: stage 1, stage 2 etc. Then pause for a moment and celebrate the completion of each stage. Pass out a brownie, lead a cheer, pat somebody on the back. Bingo! You've just injected episodes into work."

"Ok," said Brad. "Not bad. What else."

"The world has two places: in here, and out there. When bad things happen in here they are a threat. I have to duck and cover or run away. When bad things happen out there, I can man the ramparts, hurl insults and take my time firing down upon its head. Nobody gets thrown in jail for unsportsmanlike conduct. No one loses their house in reality because they lost a house in Monopoly. In play, the bad things occur out there, not in here, which make them a challenge, not a threat. So I can react heroically rather than cowardly."

"Which is okay," said Brad, "until I point out that folks really do get promoted or fired based on what they do at work. Everything happens 'in here' at work."

"Yeh, well that's *your* fault, Brad. It ain't perfect, but you can move play 'out there' by doing three things.

First, teach your supervisors to take the heat for their subordinates. Stop throwing them under the bus at every opportunity.

Second, have your supervisors separate criticisms about work from criticisms about the person.

Third, teach your supervisors to praise in public and criticize in private. Together, those three things start to build a safe 'in here' here."

"Hmmm. I don't know … it might work. What else?"

"There is no obligation to play. Folks can come and go as they please."

"Oh yeah. Like that'd work. Brother, if you don't work, you don't get paid."

"Yeah. You and I both know that you can't tell employees to work only when the urge strikes them. However, by introducing flexibility into the choice of sales territories, procedures, schedules, techniques and hours, the essence of free engagement can be approached. It ain't pure play but it's a lot closer to it than you are now."

"I'll grant you that. Okay, everyone is bathed in safety now. Is it play yet?"

"Only half way there. Without stimulation, the safety stuff leads to inertia. You become a slug. To create play, you've got to light a fire under folks. That's why play is ultimately *always* about power. I wish to score a touchdown, you wish me not to. The Martians wish to eat me, I wish them not to. I wish to achieve par, the golf course wishes me not to. In one way or another, play involves getting others to do something they would not otherwise have done, or, to do something oneself in spite of resistance.

"If you watch a child wash dishes you will note that the job clearly carries the drudgery of work until they envision the sink as a setting for naval battles and thereby make it play. Those dirty dishes become the tools of power in a battle for world dominion."

"I've seen it a hundred times. You're right. You're right. BUT, if I empower the inmates, they take over the asylum."

"The power relationship between you and them isn't really the issue here. Their need is simply to have power over something. Consequently, just about any target will do, as long as it's relevant. Heavy advertising increases a sales rep's power relative to buyers. Flex hours give employees power over their own schedules. Some firms allow every assembly line worker the authority to stop production for quality control problems, granting major individual power over the product and the production process. At a minimum, the power issue reverts back to a useful management cliché - always match authority to responsibility. Again, it's not pure play, but it gets you closer to it. "

"OK. I see that but …"

"Inmates running the asylum? Brad you *want* your employees to take over the company."
"I do?"

"Yeah. You do. That's when it becomes self-sustaining. That's when you can step back and use it like an asset, instead of carrying it around on your back. You can step away from it and pursue another dream. You can live in the Bahamas. You can sell it. Getting your employees to take over is a good thing, Brad. Not a bad thing."
"Oh shit" he muttered to himself. "Fuckin' A. Yeahyeahyeah. No. You're right."

"Just do it by evolution, not revolution. By delegation, not abdication."
"Yehyehyeh. I got it igotit."

"As part of that, stop squashing individuality. The second ingredient of stimulation is personal strategizing. . Even in highly structured play, such as football or basketball, players still exercise a high degree of individual strategizing in terms of split second decisions and specific executions. Give 'em their head. You focus on the beliefs. Yes, there is an end zone, it's down thatta way. And we score 6 points every time we get there. Go."

"Just keep pointing them in the right direction?"

"Yep. And make that end zone the most important thing in the world. Everything else becomes petty in comparison. Status, parking places, who looked at whom sideways; it all takes a backseat to getting to the end zone."

"OK. Aim at the end zone, make it the most important goal. Got it."

"Not yet but almost. In most play, the outcomes are very certain - chips, points, victory, defeat - but the attainment of them is uncertain. However, for most employees, work is the opposite. The attainment holds no uncertainty (if I push the button, the machine will operate); however, the end results are so invisible or detached from their actions that there is great deal of uncertainty about what the outcomes really are. The final ingredient of play is you've got to manage the uncertainty."

"Aha!" spouted Brad. "The first circle of hell."

"Actually, the second. But you're right on target."

"I can do this one myself, Doc. I need to give my folks the tour."

"The tour?"

"Yeah. The tour. Ford Motor Company discovered that giving workers the plant tour taken by tourists suddenly drew a connection for the widget popper at station 367 between her work and what rolled off the end of the line. It also led to a considerable number of ideas on speeding up the production process."

I liked this. He was good. "Is that it?"

"In your dreams, old man. There was a supervisor at the naval shipyard when I was working my way through college who held a 1-hour seminar on the shop floor every month called 'why we do what we do.' The answer was always the same – 'to sink #$!@ Commies, 'cause they'll take away our booze and the best women when they take over.' Simplistic, chauvinistic and paranoid. Also, terribly effective. His guys worked their butts off."

"Congratulations. Now put all these pieces together and you've got play."

"Not bad, Doc. Not bad. So let me sum up our day," he stood. "Kick their butts. And teach them to play."

"Yeah," I said. "It's called tough love."

Chapter 10
I, ME, MINE

He showed up in a foul mood. You could see it in the way his head descended into his shoulders, like a turtle preparing for battle. Turns out he'd taken a few steps backward at the office and home as well. His employees were, according to Brad, surly. And his wife had cut him off and asked him to sleep on the couch. "The piss ants are swarming and I'm about to eradicate them all, Becky included."

"Piss ants?" I inquired.
"Yeh – piss ants. Little insignificant shits that think more of themselves than is realistic."

"Becky, too?"
"Yeh, you as well."

"Okay. Do you feel this way about all of us for the same reason?"
"Yep."

"Why?"
"Because nobody does what I tell them that's why."

"Okay, fair enough. We'll discuss the case of wives and counselors in a minute. But for now, let's focus on employees. Question: why should your employees do what YOU tell them to do?"
"Because I own the fucking..."

"Yeh, I know it's your company. Nobody disputes that you have some type of legal claim to the compliance, if not outright obedience of your employees. But frankly, that's the weakest of all possible reasons."

"What?"

"First and foremost, because it takes everybody's eye off the ball. You want to focus on outcomes, the "What" --- remember? Pulling rank does nothing more that force everybody to look at the "How" the nitpicky details of inputs and process and protocols. In addition to getting on your hands and knees begging for a union, this approach is just wrong on so many levels."

"Union, my ass," sputtered Brad, "Those bastar…"

"Brad – that's not the central issue right now. So let's focus on what is --- the almighty "I". When should it hold sway? If your idea, plan or procedure is demonstrably superior than all the competing ideas, then they should do what you tell them."

"Damn straight."

"But make sure yours is demonstrably (with facts) better than the others. Number two - if your knowledge - of the product, market, and/or competition – is superior, your opinion should hold sway. In addition, if your luck is consistently better than others, your opinions should hold sway, because it probably ain't luck. It's instinct."

"I have that in spades. Why don't they listen?"

"I'll get to that in a minute, Brad. For now, realize this --- if your idea is more in alignment with the firm's strategy, mission or values than the others, your idea should hold sway. And yours always should be, since you control mission and values."

"Yeh"

"Look, here's the bottom line Brad. The rest of the world flat doesn't care about your superior position relative to your subordinates. It only cares about the outcomes you produce, for _them_. Is your product better, cheaper, more durable, prettier --- you know – better? If not, who cares about you?" He shifted his weight uncomfortably. "You need to look beyond your peasants. Keep your eye on the prize."

"What we're talking about here," I continued, "is the old fashion concept of being worthy of the mantle of leadership. It has to be earned, not bestowed, and definitely not bought. It comes from your consistent - day-in, day-out – dedication to the welfare of the team. That's why winning, profits and fame make the leader's position easy. They confirm his worthiness to lead. He knows it and relaxes into the role. His subordinates know it and confer on him the right to command, which matches the burden they place on themselves – the obligation to comply. The trick, of course, is how to keep all these relaxed rights and obligations going when the economy turns sour, or the firm hits a dry streak."

"Like now? What am I supposed to do when everything hits the fan?"

"That's when something like the milk of human kindness can be your ace in the hole. Here's a flash – if you care for people, they tend to care for you in return. If you're nice to them, ditto. If you are fair with them, ditto again. And so it goes.

"And if you kiss their ass, they'll kick you in yours."

"Not quite, Brad. In fact, as the boss you actually get some grace. Most of them will continue to like you and be loyal to you even if you treat them as pasture pastries. By virtue of your simple existence, you are what keeps them out of the 4th circle of Hell, remember? They'll suck up to that E ticket ride even after it turns sour. That's why even the worst dictators still retain a core of rabid supporters, no matter how evil they have been. Eventually, most followers will abandon you, if you are consistently terrible to them, but it takes a surprisingly long time for that to happen."

"Yeh. Like about 5 minutes."

I'd about had it by this point. "Brad, this little phenomena is the only reason you still have a business. --- or a wife. You've treated everybody like shit since the day I met you, and the only reason any of them have stayed with you is because the devil you know is better than the one you don't. But you're running out of time, and I suggest you clean up your act before you lose it all – starting with your wife."

Silence. A stillness so profound I could hear _his_ heartbeat. Neither of us moved for 5 minutes. We just locked eyes and stared straight through one another.

I broke the silence. Yeh, I know it violates the rules of the stare-down. First guy to flinch loses and all that. But I don't have time for those games. Besides, I had overstated my point just to hurt him. I'd momentarily lost the moral high ground. So I broke the silence. "It isn't a free ride, Brad. Nature plants basic checks and balances in our reptilian brain. It provides natural limits to the power of any other person. The first of these is the concept of domain. As long as you stay within its boundaries, you can get away with a lot. But step outside it and bam! – You hit a brick wall. Your folks work for you. You pay them a check every week or two. You have a time clock. When they're on the clock, their backsides belong to you – they are in your domain – and they know it. You can assign arduous and stressful tasks, make up cockamamie quotas and unreasonable job descriptions, set unrealistic deadlines – you name it and they'll do it. Because they recognize your moral authority to do so." He got up and started to pace the room.

"Now try an experiment," I suggested, "Stick your head out the window and yell at some stranger on the street to do the same things - and what happens? You'll probably receive the third finger salute. Why? Because he's not on your payroll – he's not in your domain."
"Duh," said Brad.

"Yeh, duh." I echoed. "Here's the un-duh, though. If you laugh it off, you're ok. But if you strong-arm him into compliance – you lose. Your ego will be stroked in the short run but you will have violated the concept of domain in front or your own employees and will have thereby breeched the moral order of the universe and proven yourself unworthy to be their leader. You'll probably spend a little time in jail, too, for simple battery.

Of course, you can have your cake and eat it too by buying the company that asshole _does_ work for, then imposing your will on him, and everyone would be fine with that. You just have to honor domain."
"OK," said Brad.

I'd scored a point, and we both knew it."The single biggest violation of domain," I continued, "is when the boss abuses folks on overtime. When they work beyond the time clock, it doesn't matter if you pay them for that extra time. That's still outside your domain. You're now in _their_ domain. So you better be extra special nice to those folks on overtime, because they will remember every slight on overtime, often for decades – and they will have their revenge. Always. So never berate someone on overtime. Honest. It's bad for *your* health, and it shoots a hole in your worthiness to lead. Big hole."

"You have got to be kidding," said Brad. The very reason they're working overtime is because they weren't organized enough or dedicated enough to get the job done in a regular 40-hour week. So I'm supposed to coddle the folks who were incompetent? This is ludicrous."

"No, Brad. This is reality. And there's even more. The second natural limit is the concept of scope – the range of issues on which folks get into the rights-and-obligations dance. They'll comply with your wishes on a whole array of issues: scheduling, bonuses, incentive programs, quotas, budgets and deadlines because they figure you have a right to set those things and they have an obligation to comply. Now try to tell them who to date, who to marry, how many kids to have, who to vote for. That screeching noise is them applying the brakes. You just violated scope. They refuse to give you authority over themselves on those particular issues. And again, if you strong-arm them into complying – you lose. You've violated an inviolate rule and thereby proven your unworthiness to lead. They will bide their time and simply withdraw their support and labor at some crucial time in the future. They may even go into open rebellion. But one way or the other, you're toast."

"I'd fire their ass if they pulled that crap," snarled Brad.

"You already have, Brad. And still they leave you high and dry – by your own admission. So tell me this, my friend. How's that hard-ass approach working for you?"

Silence. Only the death-glare moved across the room.

"Brad, that glaring thing only works on 3rd graders. Put it away. The last limit on your power is something called weight. Basically it comes down to "when I say jump, they say 'how high'". It goes to how much you can demand of a person. You can get them to travel once a month, maybe even once a week, maybe even everyday – for a while. But not all the time. At some point you demand too much and they just sit down. Sorry, but no. Those who can leave, will. Those who can't, will start sabotaging machinery or flight schedules or auto maintenance in order to avoid complying. That's because you violated weight. Again – you violate one of these three limits and you're toast. You prove yourself unworthy."

By this time he was standing in a corner hugging himself with both arms and rocking back and forth. I continued, "Realize that all three dimensions change over time. The definition of domain has changed over the years, as has scope and weight. If Henry Ford were alive today, he would no longer be able to regulate your choice of spouse, as he did back in 1933. But he could, once again, regulate whether or not you smoke in the privacy of your own home, on your own time. Interesting how these things go isn't it?"

"Fascinating," spat out Brad.

"Okay. So much for the lesson," I said. "Why don't you tell me what's going on, Brad?"

"What the hell is this crap about being unworthy to lead? I own the damn company. I'm the one that took the risks. I'm the one that sacrificed absolutely everything to this company. I'm the one who takes it on the chin every time something goes wrong. I'm the one who lives with all the uncertainty and does it all by my fucking self. So why am I the only one who doesn't have any authority? Answer me that one, Genius."

"Brad, it's time for you to go."
"We just started."

"No. We just finished. You don't get to attack me. So we're done for the day. Call me if and when you decide to behave yourself."
It was my office, but I left. I make it a sacred rule not to hit clients, and I was about to violate that rule. I'm not sure how long Brad stayed. Didn't really care, either.

You see, I have I-me-mine issues as well. And he had pushed a couple of *my* buttons.

Chapter 11
TELL

Becky called me that afternoon. "Have you seen Brad since your morning session?" she asked. "He never showed up at work. And he hasn't been home either. I'm worried."

"I kicked him out," Becky. He crossed the line with me, and I was also worried that anything further would cause him to bust a blood vessel. I'm a bit worried myself. Did something happen this past week that I should know about?"

"Yeh. Are you sure you want to know?"

"Absolutely," I said.
"No, really. Are you sure?"

"I am. Why the mystery."
"He tied me up last night. Pounced on me at about midnight, slapped me when I resisted, tied me to the bedposts and essentially raped the shit out of me. Twice. At first he was enraged, growling over and over that no one would ever tell him 'No' again. After the 2nd time he just sunk down beside me on the bed and cried his eyes out. I lay there trussed like the Christmas turkey for at least an hour with his head on my belly and tears running down my abused womanhood. All I could do was coo him words of comfort and hope to God he'd untie me before he stroked out completely."

"Are you okay?"
"I'm fine. Except for a lost husband, I'm terrific."

"You're right," I said, "I didn't want to know that, Becky." We shared a disheartened chuckle. "Has he ever done that before?" I asked.

"Not even close," she said.

"Any idea why, and why now?"

"Yeh, I do now. I talked to Richie Flackner, his Vice President. Brad got into a shoving match with one of his floor supervisors two days ago. The guy is the on-site organizer for a union. He thinks they've got enough votes to call for a union election and he shut down the shop floor for 30 minutes so they could make the announcement to Brad en masse. He fired them all, on the spot. Every last one of them. At which point the supervisor introduced some government guy that said no one could be fired for union activity. That's when Brad lost it. He decked the government dweeb and hit the supervisor with everything he's got. But Brad's just an ex-swimmer. The supervisor played tackle for Clemson. So the supervisor didn't budge. At which point Brad just started pushing him like a side-by-side freezer and fridge. Lots of grunts, but no movement."

"And…" I prodded her.

"And he spent 7 hours at the county jail on charges of assault and battery. He's out on bail. Pillar of the community. Not a flight risk. The whole litany – right out of Perry Mason."

By this time, of course, I was about ready to turn in my diplomas and counseling credentials. I had clearly failed Brad this morning. First rule, go where the client is. Deal with their stuff first, then get them back on the therapy path. I had bulldozed right past a clearly distressed client, racing my way to excellent – but ultimately wasted -

teaching points. "I am so sorry, sis. I blew this one. I did him more harm than good today. Worst thing is that I literally abandoned him in his hour of need. I feel awful."

"Who the hell cares what you feel like? Get out there and find my husband!" said Becky.

"Yeh, right." I responded. "I know where he probably went." I paused and pondered for a moment ... then committed, "If you don't mind me asking, how was it?"
"What?"

"The sex."
"Tied up? It was actually pretty good. That was the most passion between us in 12 years. All the more reason to find him. Go."

"I'm on it." I hung up and walked out the door. Brad's a Lutheran. Chairman of the church. Been active his whole life. But since a Lutheran is just a wanna-be Catholic, Brad had always been drawn to the smells and bells of the mother church. I went straight to St. Bartholomew's, the catholic church a block from Brad's factory. Stood in the back for a full 15 minutes to let my eye's adjust to the dark. Then I saw him kneeling motionless in a pew up front.

I sat down beside him, and after a minute or two put my hand silently on his shoulder. "You're not alone, Bubba." I said. He tilted his head to one side, then slowly shrugged his shoulders and pulled himself up to a sitting position beside me.

"Maybe not," he said. "How'd you know?"

"Where? You screwed up big time this week. On top of years of little screw ups. If ever you're gonna be in need of the Almighty, I think today's the day. You know where he lives. So do I."

"But this isn't my church."

"Yeh, I know. But yours doesn't use prayer candles. When life is falling apart, you're the kinda guy who wants to do something. It ain't much, but lighting a candle is doing something."

"So's confession," said Brad.

"No kidding?" I responded. "How was that?"
"Not bad" said Brad. "About like a session with you – but shorter."

I chuckled. "I'll have to do better. But right now I need to do a little confessing myself. I let you down today, Brad. I didn't stop to realize how badly you were hurting. It was my fault that the whole thing ended up being **a** fuck-knuckle. I am truly sorry."

"Sheeeit, Doc. Listen to you. You're not that important. We both screwed up. I gotta mouth. I shoulda interrupted and told you that my world had fallen apart this week. My bad. So forget about it. Besides, you were unknowingly narrating my life, and my week. That's what made it so infuriating. You knew what was going on – without knowing what was going on. If it was that predictable, I should have been able to avoid it. I made such a mess of things."

"I know."
"And Becky."

"I know. Yeh, she told me."
"Have I lost her too?"

"Don't think so. She kinda' liked the passion."

"That <u>was</u> good," he smiled sheepishly.

"But if you ever hit her again ..."
"I know. Never. I swear."

"Yeh, let's get out of here," I suggested. We did. It took us 20 minutes to amble the 8 blocks to my office. "I cleared the rest of my afternoon," I said. "Would you like to sit a spell? We can talk – or not - at your pleasure."
"That would be nice," he said. "I'm really tired." He sat down and removed his sunglasses so he could rub his eyes. When he looked up, I was shocked to see that both of them looked like open wounds – bright red, with little gummy deposits on the outer corner of each. "If you don't mind, I'll just catch 40 winks here." He was asleep as he uttered the last word. I called Becky and let her know I'd found him and what his condition was. She shared my concern about his eyes, and said she'd contact his doctor and email me his response.

I busied myself with paperwork for the next hour, then he woke up, fresh as the proverbial daisy.
"Did I just doze off, here?" He asked. "I'm sorry. Where were we? OK, you'd just finished with the limits to power and their affect on my moral authority to lead, right?"

"Yeh, right," I said.
"Okay," said Brad. "That leaves one last word to consider – then we're done."

"You okay, Brad?" I asked.
"Yeh, I am. Feel great. Why?" His eyes had cleared up remarkably. Just a tad bit of pink in the right one. This was just too quick of a turn around. "If I recall correctly, the last word is 'TELL', isn't it?" he asked.

"Yeh. What? Yeh. Tell. That's right. Tell."
"Communication."

"Yeh."
"How do they know what I want them to do?"

"Yeh." I wasn't hitting on all pistons. Something wasn't right.
"Luther had it right you know." said Brad.

"He what?"
"He had it right." repeated Brad. "Question – how do you know the will of God?

"I don't know, Brad. Is this a trick question?"
"Luther didn't joke," intoned Brad. "You know what God wants you to do because:
- One - it is written down
- Two – it's written down all in one place – <u>The Bible</u>
- Three – it's written about at length, in considerable detail
- Four – it is consistent with everything else we know about God

He was good, pink eye and all. "So, Luther ruled out secret personal messages - personal revelations," I said, "as well as unauthorized source material, out of context snippets and obviously made up BS. Luther was a sharp cookie."

"Hell of an executive, you mean," said Brad. "No wonder his reformation held together when most of the rest of them have fallen apart. He made sure they had a core. Lutherans knew what to do. The others were wandering in the wilderness. How come I never saw

this before? Luther pioneered the policy handbook."
He shook his head.

"You got one?" I asked.

"Yeh," he guffawed. "In name only. I haven't made an addition to it since we came out with our harassment policy in '98. My folks don't know 'the will of Brad'. I haven't been writing things down, clearly, at length and in one place. Not to mention, that my mood swings make <u>me</u> so inconsistent that my words have nothing to be consistent with. Damn. A 16th century monk knows more about running my company than I do. And he's been dead for 500 years. Damn."

He smiled the smile of a man who'd unlocked a lifelong mystery, only to find how simple it was – sheepish delight. Then he just went blank and kind of collapsed in on himself. It took about 15 seconds in all, then he was out like a light. But his breathing remained steady, along with his pulse.

Becky emailed. The doctor said not to worry as long as his pulse was below 90 and his blood pressure below 150/100. Just bring him around tomorrow for a check up. We decided to keep him at my office as long as he wanted to stay, but I asked her to stop by in an hour or so, just to be available for the ride home.

Forty three minutes later he popped right up again. "I don't think that's the whole solution, though" said Brad.

"What's that?" I asked.

"Simply writing things down," said Brad. "I actually do that pretty well – I just do it by email instead of putting them in hard copy."

"Do you label your policy statements as such?" I asked
"Ah no, what do you mean?"

"Simply label them. Big bold headline at the top of the page –"Policy # xxx" with the date. It tends to cut through the clutter."

"That's a great idea, Doc. Can I borrow a pencil and some paper?" He started to rifle through the stuff on my desktop. "But you know, even if I did that, I'd still have problems. It's like I'm speaking a foreign language."

"You are. You've got to remember to pearl two before you knit one."

"You what?" he laughed.

"Pearl two before you knit one" I repeated. Any one who's knit a scarf knows that's a standard pattern. So the expression, to anyone with half a brain, means to do things the traditional way."

"To whom?" he continued laughing.

"To 57% of your work force. The ones with boobs. Most of them learned to knit as little girls."

He stopped laughing. "Good point."

"It's as though every one has a separate language, even though we all use the same words," I said, "because each of us encodes and decodes those words and phrases to mean something a little different."

"Because, because, because." Brad interrupted "because (he got it) each one of us has a different life experience. I was never a little girl. My female employees never played football. I never gave birth. They never had an embarrassing erection. I never had a period. So women really do speak Venusian, while I speak Martian."

"Yep. And some of your folks, men _and_ women, speak republican while others speak democritian. Some, Rotarian. Others Optimist. And still others – Masonite. It's like going to Rome every time you say good morning, much less when you try to communicate something complex – like a marketing plan. And we know that when in Rome -----"

He missed a beat but I could see the wheels turning, "… do as the Romans, ah think Roman thoughts, talk like a Roman. I got it. Speak Latin! When in Rome, speak Latin." He beamed.

"So when you want folks to show some initiative, don't write 'show a little initiative' because nobody knows what the heck that means. That's Owneranian, not Latin. You've got to translate _your_ language into theirs or there is no hope whatsoever. Describe what initiative is – in their language. What does it look like, feel like, taste like. How will they know when they're showing it? How will you know when they're showing it? How will they know that you know? Break it down. Use small words. Put it in a linear progression ... if→then→if→then."

Brad walked around a bit. "This is good stuff, Doc. But it's still not going to break through to them. Not all of them, anyway. How 'bout if I show them, you know - demonstrate, role model, share, I don't know – explain, paint a picture? What am I looking for here?"

I ventured, "Sounds like teaching to me."

"Teaching! Bingo! That's it! Teaching. Yeh. That's what I was looking for. That goes beyond simple telling doesn't it?"

"Sure does," I smiled.

"But that's not all," said Brad as he paced the office. "We, I mean I, could also communicate by asking questions. I read that's better than simply telling. You know, probing questions. Investigation. Research. That thing you do, Doc. When you guide me down the primrose path, one question at a time."

"The Socratic method," I said.

"Yeh the Socratic method. I call it being the manipulative listener."

"Ha!" I laughed. "That's actually a good description.

He played around with some of the educational books on my shelf. Then turned to ask, "So how do we learn things, anyway? I mean that's a pretty amazing process isn't it?"

"Yes it is," I walked to the bookcase. "Amazing may not actually be a strong enough word. Everything that we think, feel and do comes from learning; formal, informal or accidental."

"Cognitive, affective and kinetic. Think, feel and do." He grinned as he slid the book back in place. "I paid attention in class. More than I knew."

"Not bad, kiddo." I grinned back. "And how do we get those inputs?"

"Geeze. Gimme a minute here." He studied his toes. "

- Um, the drill method, what is it – ah 'Rote'." He held up one finger.
- Then a second "or experiential, or via dialogue" two more fingers "and/or case study." He held up a handful of fingers and laughed

"That's all I got, Doc. How many did I miss?"

I patted him on the shoulder, "Outstanding work. I'd add only 'enculturation'. There's some debate, but I think it's a stand-alone phenomena. Other folks would also list observation and comparison, but I think they're just mechanical methods that fall under one or all of the items you've already listed. But don't get tied up too much in the academic fine points. Stick to the basics. Mankind is hungry for knowledge. Even Joe six-pack wants to learn. Just put people and information in close proximity to one another, and Mother Nature takes care of the rest. Look at everything you've retained."

"Yeh, but how do you translate that learning into performance? See that's the rub for me, and thousands like me. How do we get better performance?"

"Short answer?" I asked. He nodded. "Okay. Post it vertical and keep score."

"That's it?" he was surprised.

"That's it. Anytime you want them to pay attention to something, post it vertical. Hang it on a wall, a coke machine a home page. Just put it someplace conspicuous where nothing can be put on top of it. Vertical is best. Then keep score. Most Americans salivate like Pavlov's dog as soon as you announce we're keeping score. Americans love competition, even if it's against themselves."

Chapter 12
CHANGE

Brad walked in without a care in the world, looking like a pie-eyed imbecile. We debriefed his week. He'd spent the past 7 days pursuing a charm offensive. He talked to anybody and everybody. He called in every chit. And it worked. The federal agent dropped the battery charges. He claimed he'd actually slipped and it was all a misunderstanding. Brad and the union organizer were scheduled to have drinks and work out the rules of engagement. Brad felt that he could calm the waters and make it all go away.

I took a breath and started down a winding path, "Here's why I asked you to ponder the question about command versus massage back in the session on getting folks to do something. It has to do with change. Humans are creatures of habit. So if your folks are already doing a specific thing, you usually don't have to ask or tell them to continue doing it. They'll keep doing it on their own. Therefore, I have to massage change, because it causes massive upheaval in the human heart. Command only works in the movies.

He nodded.

"Short of an immediate crisis, commands don't work. Even dictators have to massage folks. They may command the peons, but they are stroking and sucking up to a whole cadre of folks that keep them in office."

"Yeah, unh huh."

"Groups survive on consistency and predictability. You can play with that a little now and then, just to wake them up and re-energize the firm, but if you take away predictability and consistency for any length of time, you usher in a state of uncertainty. And that, as we have already learned, is one of the 3 circles of Hell. So --- if you really want your entire staff to go postal – guns and the works --- institute your changes via command. Go ahead. And call me when you hit a rough spot."

He laughed a little.

"Look at it this way, Brad." He focused a bit at the mention of his name. "Change may be an event, not a process; but the embrace of that change is most definitely a process, and not an event.

The problem with embracing change is change itself. That's because change equals death. If you miss that point you don't know squat. The old has to die, so that the new can take its place. That means folks have to go through the whole mourning process for the old before they can embrace the new. I put them on the whiteboard.

> *Denial*
> *Anger*
> *Bargaining*
> *Depression*
> *Acceptance*

When bosses create change by command, their folks tend to get stuck in one of two phases: anger or depression. And they go through that each and every time. So the anger and depression keep getting stockpiled. And then we act surprised when there are labor problems."

"I've done that."

"Yeah. For about 20 years."
"Yeah …… I've made a mess here, haven't I?"

"Maybe. If you help your folks grieve for the old, their acceptance of the new will be less painful --- *if* they like the new. If they don't, well then you've got a far more complex problem to deal with, but frankly, that's not where most change goes wrong. The new order is generally as good or better than the old order. So the pain usually comes from how we institute the new order, not from the new order of things, itself."

"Wait a minute," said Brad. "I'm a little befuddled. What is it you're saying?"

I exhaled. "Change can originate from any one of four locales; from above or below, or from within or without. The only one we like is the change that comes from within. We trust our own motives. We know our own needs. Everything else is an insult to our sense of autonomy and dignity. It is an affront to common sense. It is an attack on the natural order of things. Absurd. Mean spirited. Bullshit, pure and simple."

"I think you're over simplifying."

"Yeah? How do you feel about unions?"
"They're fucking bullshit!" he exploded.

I held up my hand. "Thanks for proving my point."

We sat and stared at each other for a silent moment. At least the imbecile had disappeared. "This is why we work so hard to internalize change, Brad. We try to co-opt the subordinates. Get them to see embracing the innovation as *their* idea. Sometimes this can be done successfully, so that folks explicitly call for the change.

"Like Obama's first campaign for the White House. It was a mandate for change, enthusiastically embraced by a majority of the voters." Even in the midst of trauma, he was sharp.

"Yeah. But more often, the best you can do is internalize the *decision* to change as the least-worst response to outside pressures. "I think this sucks, but it sucks less than …"

"I got it," he said. "So how do I do this change massaging? I got a lot of changes that need to be made."

I was wrong. He wasn't getting it. "There are about 6 libraries full of opinions and data on change. It's all good and useful, but they all come back to these two points
1. Help them bury the dead
2. Help them make peace with external forces

If you are patient with the human heart and if you keep your eye on those two points, things tend to work out pretty well, if they like the new thing."

"You're repeating yourself, Chief. So I'm gonna guess that this is important. What, exactly causes people to like the new order of things?"

"There are five major reasons, Brad.
1. Relative advantage - the innovation is demonstrably better than the old thing.
2. Compatibility –the innovation assimilates into their lives easily and well
3. Simplicity – the innovation is easy to master and use
4. Flexibility - the innovation is easy to adapt and experiment with

5. Observability – the previous advantages are obvious"

"Okay, I'll buy that," he said.

"Good. Now let's look at one more issue. You remember back when we were talking about beliefs driving behavior and behavior driving performance?"
"Yeah"

"Well there is one belief that makes all the difference in the world when it comes to change. It is the belief that we have only one reason for existence; we make our customer's life better. When you firmly believe that little truism, the way you view change is changed. "It doesn't matter if the innovation is inconvenient for you – if it is more convenient for the customer. You live to serve. That's what the end zone looks like, Brad. That's why you preach it."

"So I fired the bitches, jailed the scammer and fined the slackers because …"

"Because they got in the way of our making the customer's life better. They caused us to take our eye off the ball. And nothing can be allowed to take our eye off the ball. Nothing."

"It would have helped to hear this sooner." He grumbled.

"You weren't ready."
"I'm part of the problem."

"Yeh. But that is always the case. You're the man. And you're the micro-managing man. You're part of everything. So, yeh, you're part of the problem."

"So how do I become part of the solution?"

"Brad. I want you to know that I have the utmost respect for you."

" Whoawhoawhoa. It sounds like you're gonna tell me I have cancer."

"It's gonna feel that way, Brad. But no, you' don't have cancer. Your company does. This union thing is not going away. You may triumph in the election to come, but either way, your company is sick ... and you are going to go through some major changes."

"Oh, God, no."

"You've been in denial for years Brad. And the last few months you've been flitting between denial, anger and bargaining. It's very fluid. Very spastic. You're not manic/depressive. The process you're going through, is."

He exhaled deeply, "So I'm not nuts? Sweet Jesus. I've thought I had Alzheimer's for the past 6 months. Son of a bitch." He cradled his forehead in his palm. "What lies ahead?"

"You're about to go into a soul-crushing depression that will only be relieved by fits of rage and/or tears. It is gonna get ugly, Brad. And there is no way around it. Brad, the big change here is happening to you – not to your company. You're the one who's going to have to adjust to a new reality. Somebody is taking your baby and molesting it right before your very eyes."

He moaned, "Oh, God, you're right. God damn them to fucking puss filled shit holes."

I reached over and gently touched his knee. "Stop it, Brad. Breath. Take a deep breath." I talked him down. We sat head to head, simply focusing on breathing and keeping a stroke at bay. "Brad, today's session was all about giving you the tools to survive what lies ahead. Realize the stages to the process. Don't fight them. If you want to survive this thing, you've got to work the process. It's the only way to get to acceptance and the ability to navigate the future."

"Doc. I can't. Acceptance is defeat. You're telling me to accept the molestation of my own child. I can't do that. I've got to fight it. Even if I lose."

"Brad, Brad. Brad. Focus here. Brad, I'm not telling you not to fight. I'm talking about your emotional reaction to the fight."

"What?" He came up wall-eyed but his eyes soon focused. "What? Keep fighting?"

"Yeh. Brad. This is the shit storm we both knew was coming. It is upon you."

"Son of a bitch."

"Yup. Son of a bitch. But it's here. And here's the thing to remember. Whether you win this thing with the unions or not, you're still gonna own this company when the dust settles. And you'll still have these same employees."

Oddly enough, this was obviously news to him. "Huh. I will, won't I? I'll be darned."

"Yeh, so you need to bleed the emotion out of this for you, Brad. Make it a functional issue. You'd prefer not to have a union, for one simple reason – you think it would get in the way of best serving the customer. But if the union comes, well then, you'll work with the union to figure a way to best serve the customer given the new circumstances."

"That's bulls ..."

"Brad. Your profanity doesn't do a darn thing for you. It clearly doesn't scare anyone anymore. And it just serves to raise your own blood pressure. So cut it out."

He inhaled for a great blue stream.

"Stuff it, Brad. I'm trying to help you here, with your company --- and trying to keep you alive. You are on the brink, man. On the brink. Pay attention."

He counted to ten, or ten thousand. I'm not sure. But his blood pressure receded a bit. At least according to the look of his eyes. "OK. Becky tells me the same thing. OK. I'll try to keep the language in line."

"Good. You're going through a double insult here, Brad, which is why your emotional swings are so massive. Not only is the change coming from an outside source. It's coming from beneath you; from your subordinates, your employees."

"So if I paid attention earlier, I have to internalize a willingness to engage with the union – not because I think it's a good idea, but because engaging with them is the least worst option for me."

I shook my head and grinned. "You dog. I wasn't sure you were processing anything I was saying. Yeh. That's right."

"OK." He straightened himself up. "I've got a laundry list of things to do. Note that the old me would have said 'a shit load of things'."

"Duly noted. What are those things on your list?"

"I've got to bury the past. The notion of company as family is dead. I gotta bury it and let it go. I gotta let go of my old way of doing things. Thankfully, you've already helped me start that process. Thanks. And I'll work on the language. It's fuckin hard though," he smiled a sly smile. "I'll work on it. I need to engage the union and my employees – straight up and eyeball-to-eyeball. I'm going campaigning, Doc. The union may win – but not without a fight. I'm gonna use that list of yours: relative advantage, flexibility, simplicity, etc. That'll give me good talking points. And here's my surprise tactics. I just decided it, right here. Right on the spot. Take it to the bank. I will continue the love offensive. I will not go back on that and I will not attack them. Come hell or high water, I'd like to go down like an honorable man."

"Are you sure?"
"Yep."
"So let it be written. So let it be done."

Chapter 13
SATAN AT THE GATE

He'd lost 15 pounds, at least. Looked 10 years older. But he was well scrubbed and had a look of schoolboy eagerness. His left eye had a blood spot on the outside corner.

"How you doing, Brad?"
"I'm fine Doc. I'm exercising more. Lost my appetite. Have the runs everyday. But I think things are working themselves out. I'll be fine. Really. But thanks for asking."

It was the same response I'd hear from pancreatic cancer victims when they were in the middle of chemo … two months before they died. Guarded hopefulness, in the face of insurmountable odds. I shared as much with him.
He shook his head and chuckled, "Yeh. It seems that way most days. But what the hell else am I supposed to do? Just give up?"

"What's your doctor say, Brad?"
"Funny you ask. I just saw him yesterday. He says go take a vacation. My blood pressure is up a bit … 128/100. Not bad, but a clear jump from what it normally was. He gave me some pills that make me pee like a racehorse every 28 minutes, and suggested I hit Club Med somewhere in the Caribbean. Also suggested I leave the cell phone and laptop at home."

"That's always good advice. But you're not going to follow it. Are you?"

"Naw. How can I? All hell is breaking loose. I need to man my post. I go down with the ship."

"Is the ship really going down, Brad?"

"Have you been sleeping over there, Doc? I'm on the verge of being unionized. Hell ye… Sorry. Heck yes, it's about to go down."

"Brad. You're nowhere near sinking. Your debt to equity is good. Return on Investment is better than average. Sales and margins are holding steady and cash flow is strong. Best of all, you've got a reserve fund that could choke a horse. You're nowhere near sinking. You're simply facing a transition that you hate."

"You sound like a democrat."

"No, I sound like a republican who's sick of Sarah Palin logic. You're letting your politics and your ego get in the way of solid judgment, Brad. You need to shake this off and get back in the game. Becky and the kids need you to. I need you to. And so does your company."

"My company hates me."

"No. Your company is indifferent to you. It's a make believe construct. A legal entity with no emotions whatsoever. Your company has never hated you. It's never loved you either. You just thought it did, during the easy years."

"Semantics. What are you getting at?"

"Stick with me for a few minutes here. You've gotten yourself into a linear logic trap." I held up my hand. "Just wait. It's an A-B-C process.
A. Something happens (there's a union at my door);
B. You make a moral judgment (the forces of Satan himself are upon me);

C. You react accordingly (your body and spirits are crushed as you prepare for death).
Does that sound about right?"

"Maybe. Where's this headed?"

"Inside that rock hard head of yours. What if Satan himself weren't attacking you? What if it's just your employees trying to get out of their own three circles of hell? That would put you and them on the same page, wouldn't it?"

His eyes rolled up to the right. He was thinking. "You touched on that a couple of weeks ago."

"Yeah, I did. Always assume that the other guy is logical, Brad. You just need to find the premise that drives his logic. You folks could all be working off the same ones –
- There *is* a hell.
- It stands on isolation, uncertainty and helplessness.
- And no one sees me or the problem.

You, yourself, have been screaming that for a year now. I imagine they've been doing the same."

"Son of a bit ... buck."

"Now if that is the case," I continued " is the world coming to an end?"

He shook his head, deep in thought.

I waited a moment, then prodded him. "Okay. 'A' was accurate, the union *is* at your door. But 'B' turns out to be a functional interpretation, not a moral one. So what does 'C' become? …. Brad?"

"Yeh. Hang on ….. 'C' becomes … 'it's a pain in the ass, but I can survive this, if I play my cards right.' "

"Does surviving depend on avoiding unionization?"

He looked at me as though my brain was flying straight out my ear. "Well, duh. Yes."

"Then you need to rethink, Brad. There are 9,732 unionized companies in this country. Only 77 of them went out of business within a year of being unionized. The facts tell us that unions kill less than 1% of firms. Facts. Not republican propaganda. Unions do not equal death. What they *do* equal is a colossal pain in the ass. Sit down." He'd popped out of his chair ready for battle. My words were obviously a call to arms. He sat back down. "I'm not in favor of unions, Brad. I just don't think they're Satan's spawn."

"Coulda fooled me," he pouted. "If you're so ..."

"Hang on. I'll get there in a minute. Let's finish the important point, first. (C) should be 'it's a pain in the ass, but I'll survive this regardless of the outcome of the union vote'. The fact is, you'll figure a way to work with the union if you lose. 9,732 have. You can too."

"The number is only 9,655. Remember, the unions killed 77 of them."

"I stand corrected. Should we ignore the fact that 13% of the companies that *don't* get unionized also die each year? Companies die, Brad. Happens all the time. But the fact of the matter is that the ones that get unionized have a better survival rate."

"I don't believe it."

"I know, and well gosh darn it, neither does Sarah Palin. But facts are facts Brad. It's just that there's a measurement artifact involved. Only the more prosperous companies are targeted by unions. It does them no good to unionize a sinking ship."

"Ahhh," he said. "So the union is an affirmation of my success."

"Yeah. It's a vote of confidence. Now let's look at the question I interrupted a moment ago. If I'm against unions, how would I suggest fighting them? Is that about right?"

"Yeah. So give."

"Well, first and foremost, go listen to your rank and file folks. Get in their face. Commit to the listening. Look at the back of their eyeballs, Tell yourself 'not yet, not yet, not yet'. Listen like a cartoon. Go watch tapes of Bill Clinton's town hall meetings. He was the best listener America has ever turned out. That man could listen shingles off a roof."

"Ok, I got it. Listen like a pinko."

"No, listen like a man who unseated an incumbent. That's the power of listening, Brad. It's a major component of pussy strategy. Your folks feel invisible. Go make them visible. Walk among the tribe."

"OK. You make a fair point." The old Brad was starting to resurface.

"What you're going to hear is that they want a 'Get out of Hell' card. They're tired of feeling isolated, confused, and helpless. And they feel like their problems have fallen on deaf ears. The saber rattling says, 'I ain't invisible anymore, asshole'."

"OK I get it. I get it. The three circles of hell. Visibility. I get it."

"I don't think you do, Brad. You make about a half a million per year right?" With perks, expense accounts etc, it's about $650K a year."

"That's pretty close."

"And your lowest paid full time employee, John – the assistant janitor - makes what, $17,000 a year? Twenty thousand, with perks."

"I haven't done the math, but that sounds about right."

"Did you know that the bottom 90% of your folks average making $32,000 a year?"

"Damn. How'd it get so high?"

"Do you know what $32,000 buys you, Brad? A mediocre 1 bedroom apartment, a used car, dining out twice a week – at Taco Bell - a movie with a date, and four drinks by yourself at the emporium of your choice. That's it. No vacation. No Christmas presents. No anniversary party."

"That's not a terrible existence, you know."

"Unless you want to get married, have kids and send any of them to college. Then things get pretty grim, real fast. The specific numbers aren't important. The relative numbers *are*, however. I want you to imagine standing in front of your rank and file; better yet, imagine yourself standing in front of the wives and kids of your rank & file. Now explain to them why, exactly, you're worth 32 times as much as John – who everybody likes. Better still, explain to them why you're worth 20 times more than their daddy and husband. And why the top 10% of the employees are worth 6 times more than daddy. Go ahead. I'll wait."

"That's why we keep that information secret," he bristled.

"And you're missing the entire point, here, Brad. Once the union gets involved that information doesn't stay secret. You've got a real problem here."

"Son of a bitch. Those fuckers are just after the money. I ..."

"They're not after the money, Brad. They're after what the money buys. Respect. Visibility. Dignity. Power. Most of them wouldn't know what to do with more than $100,000. It's not the money. Money is a surrogate for other things."

"It *is* the money."

"I'm not getting into a pissing contest with you Brad. Do you want my help, or should we call it a day?"

"No. Go on. I've spent the nickel. Gimme what you got."

"They want to know that incomes are proportional to the worth of each guy's inputs. You're not the problem. They recognize that owners take an enormous personal risk and therefore deserve an enormous reward. You live with the immortals. You're off the grid. The problem exists with the gap between your top 10% and the rank and file. Now they're comparing mortals and mortals. And your top 10% average 10 times more than poor old John over there pushing his broom. That's where your problem exists. Why are they worth that much more? Essentially, everything comes down to an issue of perceived fairness."

"It's a PR problem."

"Yeah. A big one. And if that top 10% behaves like a bunch of jerks, it's an insurmountable problem. If, however, they're highly competent and have superb emotional intelligence, the problem starts to evaporate. So the question becomes how does your top 10% treat the bottom 90%. Do they keep them in hell, or do they help them out?"

Silence. ... "I don't know."

"I'd make that your chief question as you wander among the tribe. And retrain your top 10% based on what you hear. If two guys call their supervisor an ass, you can dismiss it as sour grapes. But if you hear it from a third, buy that super a saddle. He's an ass. Either retrain him or get rid of him."

"You're kidding? You want me to turn my top 10% into gophers and message carriers up the ladder for my rank and file?"

I would have thwacked him on the forehead for a comment like that during calmer times. Instead, I just laughed. "Abso-fucking-lutely you numb nut. What could be better than a firm with a bottom-up communication flow? If each of your top 10 is an advocate for his/her people, your staff meetings suddenly become meaningful. There's pushing and shoving under the backboard. Energy. Conflict. New ideas. Creative solutions. Growth in the market place."

He started to say something then didn't. He thought for a moment. "It goes back to that love is a verb stuff. Is that what you're saying?"

"Go out and act like you know how to love," I purred.
"What a bucket of horse piss. That's the lamest union-busting strategy I ever heard."

Chapter 14
POWER

As it turns out, Brad drank the horse piss. Not all of it, but enough. He walked among the tribe. He listened like Clinton. He felt their pain. He suffered his own. He spoke to them like Reagan, himself. Homespun, sincere, self deprecating. Uncle Brad, sharing ultimate truths over the backyard fence. He learned from his rank and file, and acted on it. He fired two supervisors out of hand, retrained the rest and shifted the mentality from jailers to advocates. Not completely. But he made a noticeable dent in things. And productivity remained unchanged, in spite of the impending union vote, which was actually a major victory for the non-union side.

> "Turns out that a little horse piss is good for you now and then," he started. "I ain't out of the woods yet, but I don't feel like I'm in free-fall anymore."

"You're welcome."
"I didn't say thank you." … Awkward pause.

"OK. Thanks for the bulletin from the front. You're coming down the home stretch. I think you need to make one final push now. So I think it'd be useful to roll out some power strategies."
"You want to do that now? Now? At the 11th hour? Where the hell was this info when I could have used it? Six months ago? "

"You weren't ready for it. You would have seen it as a gimmick. It would have blown up in your face."

"That's a condescending crock of shit. You don't have the right to make that decision."

"Beg to differ, Brad. My secret knowledge. So I'm the only one who *does* have the right to make such decisions." We glared at each other for a moment or two.

"OK. Am I ready for it now?"

"Maybe. We'll see. But if you don't get it now, it'll simple be too late. So here we go. The secret to power is this. You can't impose it on anyone."

"That's a new one."

"Isn't it, though. They have to give it to you."

"And why, prey tell, would they do that?"

"To avoid pain, to attain gain, or to find meaning. That's Freud, Allport and Frankl in one sentence."

"Shrinks?"

"Every single one. The Troika."

"OK. Keep it out of the clouds. What do you mean?"

"I mean that power, like love, is an exchange.
- I give you something (say, power over me and my family);
- you give me something in exchange (ie, another 10 minutes of life, a salary, security, whatever).

There you have it. But if I'm not willing to give you that power, you can never ever, ever take it from me."

"If I had a gun I could."

"Not if I weren't willing. You'd kill me and then what would you have? Ever try to exercise power over a pet rock? It's a joke. It's inert. So is a corpse."

"Yeh. But everyone else would certainly jump into place."

"They probably would. Each one willingly trading power for life. That's why Hitler said that terror is the chief tool of the state."

He rubbed his left eye. "Short of a gun, what do I use?"

"Several things. Rewards are effective. You promise folks a payoff if they comply. Punishments also work. You threaten to wail on them if they don't. And get this, the great thing is that once you establish a pattern of rewards, withholding them can be the severest punishment. The good cop/bad cop game."

He looked at me out of his right eye. "That's it? I'm going to sway a factory full of adults with the stuff that sways children? They'd laugh me off the stage. Come on, Doc. Gimme something I can use."

"Don't underestimate the obvious, Brad. That's what you were doing when you fired the bitches, jailed the scammer and fined the bowlers." He was getting oddly agitated.

"There's also the one you've already established – celebrity power. People comply because (a) they like you, (b) they want you to like them, and/or (c) they want to be like you. It's how Bono got to be TIME magazine's Man of the Year – for his work on environment and poverty. He had no expertise on those topics, and didn't do a lick of work on them personally. He was a rock star, for God's sake. But he leveraged his celebrity into massive public support, which altered the actions of governments. You've had that power base for years, and your Ronald Reagan campaign this past month has been a tour de force. Bravo."

"Yeah. It has worked well. I've been real happy with that. What else?"

"Push the natural order. Common sense tells every human that someone has to be in charge. The battle is usually over who. Fortunately, America adopted capitalism as the core of our cultural ethos. So we acknowledge that the guy who owns the place has the right to command, and those of us who work for him have an obligation to comply.

"I don't think you're making the most of that. Talk about the burden of leadership. Talk about the need to make tough, unpopular decisions. Talk about your guiding light – everything for the betterment of your customer. Talk about the need for us all to sacrifice to that higher calling – a life of service. People love a call, a quest, a vision, a mission. Give 'em the big picture stuff. Reagan's city on a hill, King's trip to the mountain top. Let the Battle Hymn of the Republic well up in the background. Push a little corn pone. It's a good diet."

> He was trying to push his middle finger through the center of his forehead. "I think you're right. The atmosphere always gets thick as molasses when I talk about home and hearth. It's good stuff."

"Do more of it. You've also got a secret weapon."
"What?"

"The secret weapon. It's that you have a secret. And you're willing to use that secret knowledge on their behalf, if they comply with your wishes. It's like a reward, once you get them dependent on your secret knowledge, terror grips their hearts at the thought of losing you. So remind them of the trail of decisions that have led to and continue to support the firm's success. Don't brag. Talk about good fortune. Useful insights. Advice from others. And don't forget to attribute lots of it to luck. Luck is more important to people than knowledge. You've got both working for you. You just need to get the word out. Spread the legend."

"Really?"

"Yep. Get the word out. Then hope that someone asks what your plans are if the employees vote in the union. Let it hang in the air. Then admit that you're not sure. You've always said you'd stick around as long as it was fun. You're just not sure if having a union stand between you and the folks you love would be much fun. Aw shucks. I just don't know fellas."

"I like that", he grinned. "Vintage Ronnie Reagan."

"Yeah, It's good. They're all good. The behavioral tools can help you as long as the structure of the situation gives you a little leeway."

"Structure?"

"Yeah. How fragmented is the other side? Are they of one mind and heart, or are they doing a lot of in-fighting?"
"There are actually two different unions jockeying for position."

"Good! Help them both stay in the game."
"How?"

"I don't know. Give each a friend inside the fort. One of your top 10% who doesn't want a union, but sure prefers yours over theirs. Feed 'em a tidbit of info now and then. Give 'em a reason to hope, and to brag."

"I like this shit."

"And monitor congress like a hawk. Anything they vote on healthcare, pensions, mortgages and foreclosures is going to affect the mindset of your workers. Be active on behalf of their issues."

I fiddled with a corner of my note pad, "Mutual interdependence is one you can't win. Your employees don't even represent 1% of the national union's membership. But the national union would represent 100% of your adversary group. They can squash you in a second. Inundate you with money and personnel. You wouldn't stand a chance. But that also means you're small potatoes and you might actually be too small to even make it on their radar. How much national and regional talent are they investing in this vote?"

"I think it's one gal, and this is her first effort. I hear grumbling that she's not very good."

"Good. Another issue is concentration of forces at the point of attack. You remember the special election to fill Teddy Kennedy's senate seat in Massachusetts?"

"Yeh. The republican came back from a 30 point deficit in the most democratic of all states and pulled out a victory by 5% . It was the political equivalent of a landslide."

"Why do you think that happened?"

"The republicans never gave up. The democrats were on autopilot. By the time they woke up, it was too late. Not even flying Obama in for a last minute speech helped. So the Democrats lost their super majority and with it, the ability to over ride a filibuster. Things ground to a halt. Concentration of forces at the point of attack."

"Never give up. Never surrender. Never compromise with the devil."

"Yeah, Brad. Reel it back in. You go that direction and you have no maneuver room. Napoleon's victories were all built around retreats and re-deployments."
"Well that ain't me. I don't retreat. I don't surrender."

"Noble sentiments on a stage, Brad. But in the trenches they can be the kiss of death. The real goal here is not to *win* the fight, but to *prevent* the fight by killing their willingness to engage. To frighten or demoralize or lull them to sleep. Concentration of force is a last ditch effort if you fail to do the other things right."
"Then so be it," sputtered Brad. "Some things are worth dying for." And he was off to the races again.

"THIS ISN"T ONE OF THEM!" I shouted at him. "Can you hear me? When you're dead, you're a pet rock. Nothing happens. You're just dead."

He'd flipped back into the anger stage. It was written all over him. Coiled like a spring. Both eyes turning bright red. The stentorian voice kicking into full throttle. "Well I ain't dead yet. And you just gave me some terrific ammo. I can do the Reagan thing. Hell, I half way believe everything I'm saying. But I own this place. It's my baby. And I will not sit idly by while they ass fuck it right in front of me."

"Brad. Slow down." He was a runaway train.

"Slow down yourself, Bubba. I got a week left. I'm going to war. The gloves are off. I am kicking ass and taking names. We're going back to basics. Back to basics." His breathing was erratic. "Back to goddamned basics. He lunged out of his chair and caught himself on the arm of mine. We were head to head. "Do you understand me?" he growled. "I will have order." He staggered to the window like a drunk doing a sobriety test. "We're going back to a command center model. Top down. They don't have the right."

It was like watching a manic-depressive on speed. He grabbed the window sill and stared into the distance. He spun back toward the room. "Why in the Hell don't these little assholes just do what the fuck I tell them to do?"

* * * * *

That's when it happened. He suddenly shifted into mumble mode,

"Oh shid, Doc. My fugging head is killing me. I neeb, oh gob ..." and he was gone. Hit the floor like a ton of bricks, and never moved. Five seconds, max. From start to finish. Full of raging life, to moved out completely.

We did all the resuscitation stuff. The paramedics tried too. But every single one of us knew, from the first moment. Tears were everywhere. Mine included.

It is a terror, in it's suddenness. But then it was completely serene, because Brad simply didn't live there any more. The rest of us were slamming things around trying to bring him back, but the thing on the floor that used to be Brad was at peace – like a vacant house.

He had come so close. Fought so many demons. Almost had it in his hand. Then life and personal history conspired to push him right over the edge. He was my best and brightest, and it was a joy to fight with him in what I suspected from the beginning was a losing battle.

In retrospect, Brad's final words summed up the entire human experience. The basics of digestion, sex, life and death. And even a recognition of the Almighty.

Goodbye, Brad. I hope we helped these guys.

*There **is** such a thing as a rabbit hole.*

Would you like to go down it?

Chapter 15
THE TIPPING POINT

Brad is dead. Folks contact me all the time and ask why. They're shocked. Flabbergasted. It makes no sense. He was doing so well. He was getting a handle on things. He was making a comeback. So why'd he die? Did I make that up? Maybe he didn't really die. Maybe he had a miraculous recovery at the hospital. Maybe, maybe, maybe.

More than one has called me a real son of a bitch, and a fraud. A couple have attacked my professional competence; if I were any good, he'd still be alive. I even had one report me to the AMA, but I'm not that kind of doctor.

Folks are convinced there is a story behind the story. As it turns out, they're right. There always is. Life is complex. Every event is the intersection of numerous stories. What follows is mine.

But hang on a second. Are you sure you want to hear it? As it is, this has been a nice little cautionary tale. Grim in places, but a nice story none-the-less. If we go any further, it becomes something yet again. You can walk away right here. Just close the book, and walk away. Or you can turn the page and see that other story unfold. Your choice.

Chapter 16
BRAD'S BLOODY EYES

I've spent the last 20 years of my life serving as personal advisor, confidante and coach to 34 entrepreneurs at any one time. Not the kind that peddle questionable goods on late night TV, or out of the back of their van; but the kind that sign over the house, and the kids' college tuition, in order to build a firm that employs 25 to 2,500 people for 15 years or more. My folks add value, to the economy and to people's lives. The last time I checked, we accounted for right around $8 billion a year in revenue. That's my clientele; my compadres.

We've been to the mountain tops together and we've wallowed in the trenches together. It's been one hell of a journey, in both senses of the phrase. We've met as a group for a full day once a month for 20 years. In between meetings I've sat down with each and every one of them for two hours to talk about the stuff that is too sensitive to even bring up to the group. For 20 years I've been doing that. I've helped them bury their loved ones. I've had a hand in saving two of their kids who were attempting suicide. I've counseled them through courtship, marriage and divorce. We've done strategic plans together, product roll outs together; chased lines of credit, auditors and deadbeats together. In short, I've become a part of their lives and I care deeply for my folks.

So when I wrote my first book on creativity, I signed a copy of the manuscript for each and every one and ceremoniously passed them out as presents. I had anticipated a steady stream of emails, texts and phone calls commenting on the book. But three months later, not a one of them had so much as cracked the darn thing open. Didn't even pretend that they had. Remember now, these are nice folks. Salt of the earth types. And they owed me. Not only that, but they also like me. At least, I think so. So this was extremely odd behavior.

At our next group meeting I confronted them on the matter. I noted their decency and basic kindness. I noted our long track record of cordiality and comradeship. I touched on the nature of reciprocal relationships. Then I asked them why no one had read the book.

Silence. Except for the shuffling of feet. Lots of visual interest in the floor. Uncomfortable silence.

> Then John, one of my best and brightest blurted out, "I'll tell you why. I got no goddamned interest in creativity. I've spent my entire adult life trying to beat that shit out of my employees."

Now it was my turn. I stood there in shocked silence and watched the rest nod their heads in silent assent. A room full of CEOs – every one a millionaire, every one a responsible executive – and not a one of them interested in creativity. It boggled the mind.

> "Tell you what I *would* read." John continued "You write a book called 'Why the Hell don't these assholes do what I tell them to do' and I'll buy that book!" Nods of assent surrounded the room.

I lost a beat while that sank in, then retorted as best I could, "That's uncanny. That just happens to be the title of the book I'm working on right now!" Laughter all 'round. But that night I came home and killed John.

I made him the main character of the new book. At least, I gave his bloody eyes to Brad. That part is absolutely true. They were, and still are, a thermostat announcing his stress level. The rest of Brad's character is an amalgam of the other 33 CEOs I work with now, plus the 29 others I have worked with over the years. I killed them/him off on page one as a form of perverse black humor – to heal my injured ego and serve as a warning shot across their bow. The message was simply this ...

> Trying to impose compliance on your folks will kill you. Giving them permission to be creative will save you both.

Nice sentiment, but you should never kill someone on a lark, not even in fiction. The moment I did, two things happened. First, it suddenly became a dead-damn serious book. Second, it wasn't the book I had intended to write. The one I'd had on the drawing boards to do was a handbook on power; how to get it, how to use it, how to enjoy it. This baby became something very different.

You see, these entrepreneurs – no matter how successful and rich – are always at risk of coming undone. Death and bankruptcy are constantly 3 months away. The stress load is enormous.

- Uncertainty is everywhere they look. What if the staff calls in sick? Or the economy does? Or a new competitor blows into town and undercuts their price by 30% because he has no overhead and the brains of a toadstool? What if whatifwhatif?
- Risk is 100% for most of them. They've signed personal guarantees for every dime of capital they've raised. So if they lose, they lose everything: their

company, their money, their personal property, the savings accounts, the cars, the toys, the country club memberships and board positions --- you name it, they lose it all.
- All eyes are on them. Lives depend on the decisions they make: every employee's salary, vendor's income and creditor's ROI; the welfare of their spouses and kids, and the community's - as the cash flows from employee to grocer to farmer and on down the line to Uncle Sam and back. One major screw up and the whole house of cards comes crashing down around them.

And on top of everything else, they are plagued by their old man's ghost muttering, "I always knew you'd find a way to screw things up, Junior." Entrepreneurs eat stress for breakfast every day, and it's usually served icy cold.

And here's where it gets interesting. The uncertainty, risk and burden means that I am walking with heroes on a daily basis.
- They press on in the face of uncertainty,
- at enormous personal risk,
- making decisions that safeguard the welfare of the nation.

As Daddy Warbucks famously told Little Orphan Annie "Courage is not the absence of fear. It's the ability to press on in spite of fear." That's why my elevator speech is short and sweet.

> *"Hi, my name is Joe Anderson, and I serve as consigliere to America's heroes."*

It's a nice grabber, but it's also the most accurate explanation of what I do. I serve as Alfred to their Batman. I get 'em ready for battle, and I sew 'em back together again when the dust settles.

So, no, there wasn't actually a Brad. And, yes, he did actually die on my office floor. No, he didn't get unionized, but, yes, the thought of it drove him to distraction. No, his wife is not named Becky, but, yes, she's put up with some relational oddities because she knows in her bones the stress Brad carries. Here's the point – everything in the book actually happened, just not all to the same person. Every action actually occurred, some of them performed by me, not my many Brads. We're all bits and pieces of Brad. That's why the book is neither fiction nor non; neither memoir nor fantasy, history nor propaganda. Instead, it is the story of my walk with heroes. I call it a novel of sorts.

> "But what the hell does it mean?" asked John. True to his word, he actually read the first 14 chapters of this book. He thought Brad was going to make it. In fact, he'd called me a couple of days earlier to gloat. I was standing on 47th street in New York City, getting ready to go see "The Lion King," when he called. He was laughing. "This son of a bitch is going to pull his bacon out of the fire, isn't he?' John chortled.

"Just read the book, John," was all I said.
> "OK. Just wanted you to know I love this shit. Bye"

> Two days later, his call was very different. "You son of a bitch. I hate this shit. Why'd you kill him off? It's like a punch in the gut."

"John, he didn't just die," I said. "He's been dead for the whole book. I told you that, back on page 1."

"I know, I know I know." Said John. "But I thought you'd give him a break - some alternative ending --- you know, saved by his secret knowledge. The whole revelation thing."

"Ignorance didn't kill him, John. Stress did."

"What in the hell am I supposed to do with that?" he asked.

"Well, did you learn anything from the story?" I asked.

"Other than to never read another one of your god-damned books?" he responded.

"Yeh."

He scratched his forehead and grimaced. "I don't know. The story got in the way. Maybe not. Yeh. I'd get a nugget now and then, but then the story would go on and I'd kind of leave the nugget behind. If you want me to learn something from it, put it on a pedestal and surround it with neon light. And for God's sake, keep it short. I don't read when I don't have to, you know."

Well John, the next chapter is for you and your bloody eyes. I hope it helps.

Chapter 17
SO WHAT WAS THE POINT?

In a nutshell, here's what the book taught us.

> Life is hard, full of
> - uncertainty
> - isolation
> - helplessness, and
> - despair.
>
> And love is the only way out.

If all you're going to take away is 6 points, those are the 6 points to take. They'll make you more compassionate, more emotionally intelligent, and ultimately, more successful.

That's it.

Of course, *on the grand scale*, I put a whole lot more than that into the book. Here it is.

1. **Most of us spend most of our time dancing along the rims of the four pools of hell,** desperately trying to stay dry. We stare into the pools of uncertainty, helplessness and isolation, knowing full well that if we fall into the intersection of the three, we will be trapped in utter despair – which is nigh unto impossible to escape and always, repeat always, akin to drowning.

2. Once we understand that, the majority of human behavior makes sense. It is a rational effort to:
- stay out of the circles,
- get back out of the circles once we've fallen in, or
- compensate for having fallen into one of the circles.

3. Leadership is, in part, the act of keeping people out of the four circles of hell --- and occasionally --- nudging them back in, so you can help them learn to get back out, or simply rescue them yourself.

4. You see, leadership centers on the use of power, not pastoral care. Pastoral care is simply one of the ways in which we can exercise power.

5. A leader has two jobs
- Define the objective
- Move the troops in that direction.

6. The four circles of hell are the biggest obstacles to moving the troops … but they are also the most useful tools for moving the troops, because …
- a man will sell his mother to <u>avoid</u> falling into the 4th circle
- but he will sell his own soul to <u>get out</u> of it himself

In between the nutshell and the grand scale is an enormous fertile field --- the "how to" field. There are literally hundreds of models, tools, cornerstones, pillars, weapons, and land mines scattered all over "How-to" field. I'm going to tell you mine. And listen up, because they are the only true and practical route through the minefield. Well … that might be an overstatement. Let me rephrase. I'd like to share my approach.

A. **Stop trying to be in control.** You will always fail, and in failing you will always heave yourself into the 4th Circle. The only surer way to commit suicide is to buy bullets. Stop that crap, or change your name to Brad.

B. **Instead, focus on exercising power.** Power is the ability to get other people to do something they would not otherwise have done. Something, not everything, not every time. Just something. It's a matter of scale. Only God hits a homer every time. Learn to live with doubles and singles. Any movement toward the goal is successful leadership.

C. **Love is the single most powerful tool a leader possesses**. Why do you think that is? Because love keeps people out of all four circles of Hell. You're not isolated if someone loves you, are you? And there is always one point of certainty in your life when you know you're loved, isn't there? And when you have someone to turn to who loves you, you ain't helpless anymore, are you? And if you are able to stay out of just one of the circles of hell, you will never be able to fall into the intersection of them all, will you? Impossible. Won't happen. So if you have a desperate need to avoid the 4th circle, and love is the single most powerful tool for keeping you out of it ---- what are you willing to do to get someone to love you? Hmmmmm?

D. Love is a verb. It is how you behave, not how you feel. Think seduction and you'll get it. When you love you listen, you lean, you mirror breathing patterns and body language. When you love, your pupils dilate, you have more eye contact, and you smile a lot more. You act like this on someone else and you will be loving all over them. And they will react for a very simple reason.

E. Humans can not stand being invisible. They know that if they can't be seen they can't be rescued, and can't be loved. And if those two things are out of reach, they know they'll be flushed down the 4th circle for sure. It's not just kids who will act up just to be noticed. Most bad behavior by adults occurs for the exact same reason. Why do you think the good guys in the movie Avatar greet each other with "I see you", hmmmm?

F. Most of the good behavior in this world is done so that you will see the doer. You see, this phenomena – like the 4th Circle Model – can work both ways. It can be an obstacle – or we can pre-empt the bad stuff and use it for good. Start noticing the people in your life. Stop dead in your tracks. Take a breath. Look them in the eye and say "I saw what you did on (fill in the blank). That was good stuff. Thanks." They will love you back. And do something else wonderful, just so you will see them again.

G. No one loves their doormat. Don't be confused. Love is not a tender, take advantage of me, strategy. Love also make demands, and enforces them. Think Teddy Roosevelt ---"Walk softly, but carry a big stick."

H. The best punishment is simply removing a reward. Get them hooked on your love then simply make them invisible again if they do wrong. Most folks will hop back in line, go out of their way to make sure you know it, and never blame you for disciplining them. Nifty trick.

I. Leadership sounds pretty manipulative. Of course it is. Companies are started in order to make a profit for the owner. They are not started in order to provide full employment or happiness for the neighborhood. In fact, the better I am at running my company, the fewer employees I will need, for any given level of production. And I do that by getting people to do things they would not otherwise do; like show up at o-dark-thirty, everyday; do the same task the same way, every day; and learn to get along with their co-workers, despite the fact that some of them are jerks. And manipulation is one of the ways we exercise that power.

J. Be their "Catcher in the Rye" – Straight forward, genuine care and affection are also part of your arsenal. Genuinely help your folks stay out of isolation, uncertainty and helplessness. Genuinely notice and care about them. What a concept – basic human decency as a sneaky leadership tactic.

K. Love only works, however, if you have more emotional intelligence than a gnat. If you are one of those folks that alienates people simply by showing up, this whole love strategy will blow up in your face. Just don't even try it.

L. If you find yourself saying "Why in the hell won't these assholes do what I tell them to do" --- buy yourself a casket. Or change your ways.
- Take the time to find out why folks do what they do.
- Delegate; don't abdicate. It changes "won't" to "can't".
- Take the time to train them (again and again and again)
- Discover who the real asshole is. A mirror helps.
- Don't overstep your limits. You're the boss, not the God.
- There is no I in TEAM --- even if *you're* spelling it.
- Stop trying to be in control. Focus on power, instead.

M. Napoleon's greatest move was the strategic retreat. Be willing to reverse field. Then run around the obstacle and attack from the flank. In short – there's more than one way to skin a cat.

N. **Be a tyrant on the big stuff.** <u>You</u> define the endzone --- where it is, what it looks like, how we're going to get there. Then, for God's sake, lighten up on the small stuff. Let your employees have some say over the inputs – subject to one proviso – it must make progress toward the endzone. Anything that takes us toward the sidelines, or loses ground is forbidden. Then challenge them to beat the water cooler.

O. **Don't make them guess.** Martin Luther's dictum for discovering the will of God was: (1) it must be written down, in one place, (2) it must be written about at length, with clear and specific detail, (3) it must be consistent with God's overall goals and behavior. Since you're no better than God, I suggest you leave the same evidentiary trail for your employees.

P. **Engage in magical thinking**. When someone tells you a thing can't be done, say "Okay, okay. Take two more days." Then give them the Steve Jobs stare and ask if there's someone else better qualified to do this thing. In short, a specific action may well be impossible, but the goal never is.

Q. **Attend the king, ignore the peasants.** Your goal is to beat the other king, not your own peasants. So stop worrying about the gap between you and them. In fact, help them get rich, because they can only do that if they make you wealthy beyond your wildest dreams of avarice.

R. Thou shalt not muzzle thine oxen (Hezikiah 9:13). Let them nibble on the grain while they're pushing the millstone for you. If you want them to take on the obligations of ownership thinking, you have to let them take on the perks of ownership as well. In short, give them a meaningful cut of the profits.

S. Stop honoring stupid. Smart is always better than stupid, regardless of what cornpone politicians say during every election.

So what should you do about all this?
It all boils down to three little cliches'…

*1. Life is a drama – <u>act</u> like you know what to do. You will eliminate uncertainty for those around you. And when they start acting with courage, some of your own **Uncertainty** will disappear as well.*

2. Life is a party, be the host. – Never eat alone. Ask a bum to lunch if no one else is available or willing. Then ask them a series of three questions that can't be answered with a yes or a no. And no matter what they say, your response is "That's fascinating. Now I'm just curious, how (or why) did that ..." You will no longer be alone. It is amazing how quickly you can kill **Isolation**.

$3.$ *Always play offense, even on defense. Defense has to be good on every play. Offense only has to be good every once in awhile. In addition, every play on offense is a chance to win the game. The best you ever get on defense is a chance to not lose the game. Playing offense puts a dent in your sense of* **Helplessness**.

Oh Yeh. One last thing

What happened to Brad's business? Like most control freaks, he'd refused to name a successor or produce a succession plan. No buy/sell agreement, no key man insurance. It was a mess, and poor Becky didn't know a thing about running a business.

But the business has been doing a bit better without Brad. Turns out Becky is a maven of emotional intelligence. She knows exactly where the end zone is. And every play they make is a step in the right direction. She took Brad's place in the CEO peer group and we are lucky to have her.

Brad, however, is still dead. Stress will kill you, folks.

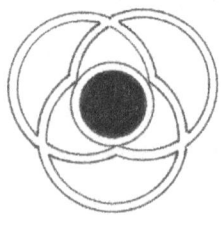

The End

The Author - *Joe Anderson,* PhD

Joe has served as personal advisor and counselor to more than 60 CEOs, controlling over $8 billion a year in sales and 3,500 employees - in large measure, via his chairmanship with Vistage - formerly known as The Executive Committee (TEC). He's been doing that job since 1995, along with occasional public speaking and a pretty fair amount of writing.

Prior to that, he successfully ran an organization himself, then went to grad school to find out why it had gone so well. He emerged with a PhD and taught for 10 years in some of the leading business schools in America; getting voted Professor of the Year at several of them. You can reach him via:

www.joeandersonphd.com

Other Books by Joe Anderson

THAT THING BETWEEN YOUR EARS IS AN IDEA: How to get one. How to use it. How to lose it when you're done. (Available at Amazon.com)
The average business needs a good, big, idea every 17.3 weeks – just to stay abreast of the competition. You know --- things like new products, processes and/or markets to pursue. But those are hard to come by because we've hemmed ourselves in by creating and enforcing a multitude of little ideas; like inventory systems, budgets, performance metrics, etc. So we forget what a good, big one even smells like, much less how to actually have one. That's where this book comes in. It will literally jump start your brain.

THE QUEST FOR TRUTH & GLORY: Creativity on the Mountain Top. (Soon available at Amazon.com)
Based on the lives of 72 people who changed their corner of the world, and thereby ours, for all eternity --- Joe uncovers a handful of traits and actions that seem to fuel and guide The Quest for Truth & Glory. The result is a handbook on how to change the world.

TO TOUCH THE HAND OF GOD: What happens when we create change? (Soon available at Amazon.com)
The single biggest determinant of American values is the Christian faith on which the majority of us cut our eye teeth. Even the atheists and agnostics among us are a product of that faith. That's good in many ways, but Christians and their ilk are usually the enemies of change, because change threatens their notion of a changeless deity. Joe posits a novel interpretation of that relationship. We do not slap the face of the Almighty when we champion change. Instead, we reach up and Touch the Hand of God.

www.ingramcontent.com/pod-product-compliance
Lightning Source LLC
Chambersburg PA
CBHW022131080426
42734CB00006B/315